MISSION TRIP PREP KIT LEADER'S GUIDE: COMPLETE PREPARATION FOR YOUR STUDENTS' CROSS-CULTURAL EXPERIENCE

KEVIN JOHNSON

WWW.ZONDERVAN.COM

www.YouthSpecialties.com

Mission Trip Prep Kit Leader's Guide: Complete Preparation for Your Students' Cross-Cultural Experience

Copyright © 2003 Youth Specialties

Youth Specialties Books, 300 South Pierce Street, El Cajon, California 92020, are published by Zondervan Publishing House, 5300 Patterson Avenue Southeast, Grand Rapids, Michigan 49530.

Library of Congress Cataloging-in-Publication Data

Johnson, Kevin, 1964-
  Mission trip prep kit leader's guide : complete preparation for your students' cross-cultural experience / By Kevin Johnson.
      p. cm.
  ISBN 0-310-24488-9 (pbk.)
  1. Short-term missions. I. Title.
  BV2063 .J56 2005
  259'.23--dc21

                                                                                    2002012153

Web site addresses listed in this book were current at the time of publication. Please contact Youth Specialties via e-mail (YS@YouthSpecialties.com) to report URLs that are no longer operational and replacement URLs if available.

Edited by Vicki Newby

Cover and interior design by Mark Arnold

Production assistance by Nicole Davis

Printed in the United States of America

05 06 07 / DC / 10 9 8 7 6 5 4 3

GO.>

DEDICATION:
TO NATE, KARIN, AND ELISE
MAY THE LIGHT OF JESUS BLAZE IN YOU FOR ALL THE WORLD TO SEE – FOR YOUR GROWTH, OTHERS' GOOD, AND GOD'S GLORY.

Acknowledgments: Thanks to Teen Missions International and the 1980 Venezuela Team for jolting me awake and aiming me down God's road. Thanks to Paul Bertelson and YouthWorks, along with Seth Barnes and Adventures in Missions for coaxing me to write my original ACTS mission prep curriculum. Thanks to Mark Oestreicher and Youth Specialties for pursuing this book. And thanks to Mindi Conradi for bringing youth missions to Peace Lutheran— and for so capably pulling together trips that alter our youth and their worlds forever.

CONTENTS

GO-V

CH.1

WHY DO
SHORT-TERM MISSIONS?

CH. 1

WHY DO SHORT-TERM MISSIONS?

Picture this:

You're a parent who is frantic to see something good happen in your church for your youth. You want them to step closer to God, bond with positive friends, and integrate with the adults in the congregation. What do you do?

Or you're a church volunteer who sees the youth you teach week after week spouting all the right facts yet showing no fruit from a tight relationship with God. They're choking on too much Sunday school. How can you grab hold of them with a spiritual Heimlich maneuver?

Or you're a rookie when it comes to working with students. Still you know God wants to use you in their lives. You're looking for ways to grow the youth you know. Where can you start?

Or you're a youth pastor worn out from trying to devise programs as enthralling as this week's hottest band, movie, or quiz show. You want to train your youth to take the next step toward God, not to expect you to produce a bigger and better program for each youth group meeting. How can you extract yourself from the contest to be voted America's Hippest Youth Pastor?

Or you're a student at the head of the your youth group pack, someone who senses there's more to following Jesus than sponging up Bible stories and doing church socials. You hate it when adults pat you on the head and tell you you're "the church of tomorrow." What can you do to make a difference in your world *today?*

Or you're a senior pastor wanting to energize what looks like a fizzling youth program. You know firsthand the struggle to be relevant without selling your soul, and you wonder how to best engage today's youth. What sort of guidance should you give your youth staff?

Maybe you see bits and pieces of yourself in several descriptions—or your situation is unique.

Yet if you've picked up this book you probably sense that all of those dilemmas share a common solution: Thousands of youth workers have found that an indispensable key to moving their students toward spiritual growth is involving them in short-term missions.

THE ANSWER IS MISSIONS

Missions. Not an expanded diet of lock-ins and wild stunts.

Missions. Not more splashy meetings laced with pricey multimedia.

Missions. Not another luxurious camp or retreat.

Launching students into short-term missions produces effects far more enduring than entertainment. It cracks opens the hearts of youth to biblical content and commands in a way that fun-and-games can't. It ignites their minds far faster than lectures. It captures the attention of youth who want to do rather than sit and learn from a book, even if that book is the Bible. It can draw jaded students into a lifetime of making a difference in the world. And contrary to the old-school youth ministry theory that says the only way to evangelize students is by luring them in with crazy events and then surprising them with the gospel, a service event can even be an entry point to meeting God.

Students who take part in short-term missions join an activity at the center of the heart of God. As they get up-close-and-personal with the purposes of God in their world, they can glimpse the God who is ultimate power, ultimate intelligence, ultimate justice, and ultimate love—the God who burst into history in the person of Jesus Christ to wrap them and their world in total care, total wisdom, total fairness, and total belonging. They see that God passionately wants them to know him and to make them a part of his plan for the world.

THE THREE BIG REASONS TO GO

If you've never done a short-term mission trip either on your own or with students, you might smell a sales job. You may have heard the enthusiastic testimonials of youth workers who have led students on trips, yet you wonder if trips actually do anyone any lasting good. If you're already signed up for a trip, you might be wondering how to maximize the event. And if you've done a short-term project and had a less-than-incredible experience, you might be asking yourself why the project didn't produce the promised results.

The good effects of plugging your students into missions aren't automatic. The effort isn't as easy as barging into your youth group and announcing that you're doing a trip to Nepal next summer. But this guide will help you pull together everything you need to ensure your trip's success—to get ready, accomplish much, and make it stick when you get home. Whether you're a first-timer or a veteran of many short-term mission projects, *Mission Trip Prep Kit* will assist you in making the most of your project.

To start, here's a big thought: While the process of dreaming up the perfect trip for your students leaves your brain aswirl with questions of where to go and what to do, you're far more likely to get to the good results you seek if you first settle a bigger question: Why go at all?

Involving your students in short-term missions is nothing less than latching on to God's colossal plan to reach humankind with the Good News of Christ. Done right, that endeavor reaps at least three huge benefits:

BENEFIT: OUR MAXIMUM GROWTH. Frankly, the growth of your students might be your pressing priority. Facilitating their growth might be your paid duty, your full-time responsibility, the heartbeat of your life. And asking what a mission trip can do for you and the students you lead isn't a selfish question—not unless you're using missions as a ruse to set up a beach bash in Cancun.

Here's why. Outreach isn't just how Jesus spread news of his kingdom and met the needs of the world at large; it's also how he trained his followers. After those followers watched Jesus minister to the crowds (Luke 8:1), he sent them out two-by-two, first commissioning his 12 closest disciples (Luke 9:1-6), then a group of 72 (Luke 10:1). If you check the biblical texts, you'll notice that the people he sent were still homing in on Christ's precise identity (Luke 9:18-20). Jesus didn't send them out because of their thorough maturity but, in part, to move them toward that maturity.

The same kind of quantum growth that Jesus plotted for his disciples occurs because students involved in outreach help usher in even bigger benefits.

BENEFIT: OTHERS' MAXIMUM GOOD. God aims to do something about the world he sees distanced from himself and mired in destruction. Early in his public ministry Jesus engaged in a set of actions that illustrate the kind of good he intends for us to replicate as we do missions: When a group of men lowered their paralyzed friend through a roof to get him close to Jesus, he forgave the man's sins and healed his broken body and called him his friend (Luke 5:17-26).

That's exactly the kind of spiritual, physical, and emotional good Jesus predicted he would bring to the world when he stood in his hometown synagogue and read a prophecy from Isaiah: "The Spirit of the Lord is on me," he said, "because he has anointed me to preach good news to the poor. He has sent me to proclaim freedom for the prisoners and recovery of sight for the blind, to release the oppressed, to proclaim the year of the Lord's favor" (Luke 4:18-19). When students imitate Christ's love for the world, they do good for others that brings people whole-life help.

BENEFIT: GOD'S MAXIMUM GLORY. Our motivation for missions starts with the Bible command to "go and make disciples of all nations, baptizing them in the name of the Father and of the Son and of the Holy Spirit, and teaching them to obey everything I have commanded you. And surely I am with you always, to the very end of the age (Matthew 28:19-20). That Great Commission tells us what to do, but often we lop off what Jesus said about why we do it: because "all authority in heaven and on earth" belongs to Jesus (Matthew 28:18).

God's greatness and majesty are one-of-a-kind awe-striking. And his goal is for everything about him—everything worth praising, honoring, and respecting—to be broadcast throughout the world. Isaiah 60:2 says, "See, darkness covers the earth and thick darkness is over the peoples, but the Lord rises upon you and his glory appears over you." Habakkuk 2:14 puts it this way: "For the earth will be filled with the knowledge of the glory of the Lord, as the waters cover the sea."

Right before Jesus headed back to heaven, he made a great prediction of exactly how and where God's glory would spread: The Holy Spirit would empower all of us to speak and act—and we would be the ones to "tell people about [Jesus] everywhere—in Jerusalem, throughout Judea, in Samaria, and to the ends of the earth" (Acts 1:8 NLT).

God isn't glorified only when individual lives are repaired or even when individuals trust in him. God's biggest goal is to build a people. God made us for friendship with himself and each other, but sin smashed that friendship. His goal now is to build a tight group of friends who belong to him—friends who honor him as their Master and rely on his care now and forever, and whose hearts beat with his compassion for all the people of the world.

1 Peter 2:9-10 puts in plain words the good that God wants to use us to do in the world: "But you are chosen people. You are the King's priests. You are a holy nation. You are a nation that belongs to God alone. God chose you to tell about the wonderful things he has done. He called you out of darkness into his wonderful light. At one time you were not God's people. But now you are his people. In the past you had never received mercy. But now you have received God's mercy" (NCV).

NO BETTER WAY TO GROW

Our growth. Others' good. God's glory. Those are great benefits, but benefits that large can be abstract and hard-to-grasp.

As a youth worker-type contemplating a short-term trip for your group, you no doubt intend for your efforts to showcase God's greatness. You surely want to make a difference in the lives of the real people you reach out to. But your immediate reason for picking up this book is likely the huge change that short-term missions can work in your kids. So check out some of the big reasons why short-term projects are so effective in growing students:

SHORT-TERM MISSION EXPERIENCES OFFER AN EFFECTIVE WAY TO TEACH AND DISCIPLE YOUR STUDENTS.
When Jesus took his disciples along as he ministered and then launched them to minister on their own, he was conveying spiritual content in the context of real life. It works the same for us: No class-

room teaching tactic has the punch of a real-life project, and a short-term trip offers a concentrated way for students to see God at work in and through them. From a purely educational perspective, mission trips are effective because it naturally yields cognitive, affective, and behavioral results—helping students learn with their head, heart, and hands.

SHORT-TERM MISSION EXPERIENCES COMMUNICATE YOUR BELIEF IN YOUR STUDENTS. In his book *The Power of Believing in Your Child*, youth speaker and former San Diego Charger Miles McPherson talks about touring the aircraft carrier USS Abraham Lincoln. As the captain reeled off facts about the multibillion dollar floating airport, Miles noticed the helmsman. Steering the ship was a baby-faced 19-year-old. If young women and men still in their teens can guide planes, target bombs, read radar, guard our national security, and put themselves in harm's way, we can trust them to be a light to the world. With a potency few other activities possess, short-term missions call students to live up to the active faith they are capable of.

Plenty of people overlook the potential of youth for accomplishing anything significant, whether teachers who baby-sit them until graduation or media that paints them as selfish rebels. Even many parents fear their children's growing maturity and puzzle over how to channel adolescent energy. When you dare youth to do their best by doing real ministry, you demonstrate gigantic faith in them.

SHORT-TERM MISSION EXPERIENCES HOOK STUDENTS ON MINISTRY—AND ON GOD. If students only know about God from week-in, week-out experiences of Sunday school and youth group, they can draw some misguided conclusions about their faith. They might think that following Jesus is all about sitting still and listening to someone drone on. And if the only place the adults of the church see youth are the week-in, week-out experiences of Sunday school and youth group, they might draw some misguided conclusions about adolescents.

For most youth, making their lives matter is high on their list of priorities. Taking part in a short-term mission project lets them make a difference in someone's life, maybe for the first time. It can jumpstart a life of service, making ministry a normal, everyday part of a student's journey as a Christian. Opening up opportunities for service, in fact, might be far more important than you imagine.

In one of the few empirical studies of why youth distance themselves from God, Dr. Bob Laurent found that teens' own most-cited reason for ditching God was surprising: their church failed to provide opportunities for significant involvement (*Keeping Your Teen in Touch with God*, LifeJourney Books, 1988). Those "opportunities for significant involvement" often revolve around apprenticing youth in real ministry—in evangelism, administration, helps, social justice, worship, Christian education, and discipleship. Students not only need more than fun and games, they want more. Mission projects are one way to give it to them.

NO ARM-TWISTING REQUIRED

Offering your youth the opportunity to take part in a short-term mission project might not awaken an overwhelming response the first time. But recruiting is infinitely easier the next time. Countless students back from well-run trips report to their parents, pastors, and peers that they have experienced all kinds of growth:

THEY AUDACIOUSLY SHARE WHAT THEY BELIEVE. For some students, merely identifying themselves with a mission team—signing up, climbing in the van, being seen as part of the group, even wearing a project T-shirt—is a huge bit of boldness. Others step out by speaking about their faith. And some stretch to taking part in proactive evangelism, talking with strangers in a winsome way.

THEY MEET PEOPLE DIFFERENT FROM THEMSELVES. Not many students sit around with their friends contemplating how to spend their spare time and come up with, "Let's go meet some homeless people—or some senior citizens—or some people of another race or religion." But that doesn't mean they won't grab hold of the opportunity if you put it in front of them. Short-term mission projects open the door to a world they might never enter otherwise.

THEY DO NEW THINGS FOR GOD. Lots of youth are never trusted with a lawnmower, much less a circular saw or a pneumatic hammer. They've never climbed a ladder or hung out on a roof. Serving God gives them the chance to contribute more than they ever thought possible. Armed with the right instructions and right attitude, they can learn to do more than we can imagine.

THEY COME INTO CONTACT WITH GOD'S POWER. Short-term mission experiences hand students opportunities to go where they've never gone before—to live in uncomfortable conditions, acclimate to strange environments, blast through new challenges. In the midst of their discomfort they experience God's comfort and protection.

THEY GAIN COMPASSION FOR PEOPLE AT WAR WITH GOD AND EACH OTHER. Short-term mission trips often take students where the reality of evil is stark and where suffering is obvious. They learn compassion for people they had ignored or disdained.

THEY HELP OTHERS TAKE A STEP TOWARD GOD. Short-term student missionaries won't likely see a whole country trust Christ because of their initiative, but they can see attitudes soften. Their work can create a fresh openness to God. And they can sometimes see individuals and even large groups trust Christ.

THEY SEE FIRSTHAND THE DIFFICULTIES FACED BY CHRISTIANS. Some short-term trips will take your youth face-to-face with the poverty, persecution, and suffering Christians in other cultures experience as a direct result of their faith. And even on trips to less hostile environments many students will meet someone who doesn't like what they're doing—and taste the rejection Jesus faced as he reached out to the world.

THEY DEPEND ON GOD. When students wander out of familiar surroundings, they can be taught to prayerfully trust God to meet their every need. Faced with real needs requiring real help, they might discover for the first time the reality and power of prayer.

THEY GAIN HUMILITY. Many students are surprised to learn they can be happy ditching their designer clothes to get grubby and do dirty work. You have a bonus as they find acceptance by their friends when they look, smell, or feel less than their best.

THEY WORK AS A TEAM. Mission trips almost always force students to try tasks they could never tackle solo. They learn what teamwork means and learn to give credit to God.

THEY EXPERIENCE GOD'S CARE AS THEY EXPRESS GOD'S CARE. As God helps participants stay afloat in rough waters, they learn that God will always be there for them—whether their trials are spiritual, emotional, or physical. They find that as they give, God fills them up with even more.

While no student learns all these profound concepts in a single trip, rare is the student who doesn't take away at least one lifelong lesson.

MAKING CHOICES

Some of the host organizations that provide ready-to-go short-term missions require little or nothing of you before you show up for the trip other than collecting money and turning in the proper forms. While immediate immersion can be a beneficial kind of spiritual shock therapy, your group may profit more from the experience with advance preparation. If you want to achieve the goals of facilitating maximum growth in your youth, doing maximum good to others, and bringing maximum glory to God, then you'll want to put more effort into the process than signing up and showing up.

The goal of this book is to help you put together an effective trip for your students, so this mission trip kit is packed full of ideas to help your group catch God's vision and power for the experience of a lifetime.

The front part of this book contains six chapters that will help you make key decisions to buff up your trip from start to finish. The back part contains plans for half a dozen sessions with your students—four for preparation before your trip, two for follow-up afterward—that will help you maximize your experience. These sessions can be condensed or expanded, conducted over a period of weeks or crammed into a retreat right before you leave.

IN ADDITION TO THE GROUP SESSIONS, *MISSION TRIP PREP: A STUDENT JOURNAL FOR CAPTURING THE EXPERIENCE* IS AVAILABLE TO HELP STUDENTS PROCESS THEIR EXPERIENCES INDIVIDUALLY.

As you progress in your planning you might choose to add meetings to sharpen skills specific to your trip. But this kit isn't meant to launch you into a cycle of endless meetings. The lesson suggestions do more than convey information; they help students practice the skills and attitudes now that they'll need for your trip and help you address areas where your group must grow if your trip is to be successful. A group that grows in these areas is more likely to have impact at its site and lasting life-change when it returns home.

READ THE FINE PRINT

Before you launch into **Mission Trip Prep Kit,** understand the assumptions built into it. They're the basic beliefs undergirding everything in this book. They're also the attitudes that bring success to short-term mission projects:

+ ALL STUDENTS ARE CAPABLE OF LEADERSHIP. Not all students crave the chance to exercise up-front leadership, but each can do something relatively well that many others do poorly—even if that gift is a hidden talent that seldom garners applause. Each can help set the pace in an area or two of individual giftedness. It's the job of adult leaders to figure out what students' gifts are.

MINISTRY IS FOR ALL STUDENTS. Involving students in any kind of ministry is sometimes regarded as an optional extra of the Christian faith, an add-on for the spiritual elite. While the Bible warns against giving new believers visible, public roles before they are ready (1 Timothy 3:6), ministry is an indispensable part of the maturing process for youth.

SERVICE CAN BE A HOT COMMODITY. Youth don't need to be dragged by the nose into service. When missions and other opportunities to serve are enthusiastically presented as a privilege of following Christ, youth readily grab the opportunity to join in.

SHORT-TERM MISSIONS ISN'T A FAD. A generation ago few youth groups had participated in mission trips. But 30 years later, thousands have. The anything-goes attitude of early mission projects has been replaced by accountability for effective use of time, energy, and finances.

SHORT-TERM MISSIONS SHOULD PROGRESS. If you're just getting started in taking students on short-term mission trips, you'll do great good just by getting involved in a weekend or week-long project relatively close to home. But over the long haul your strategy of involving youth in missions will go stale if you do the same basic trip year after year. At some point you'll need to think hard about how you can arrange multiple opportunities for your students. You'll want to keep first-timer trips available but allow your students to launch into more challenging trips as they mature.

SHORT-TERM MISSIONS DONE BADLY CAN BECOME A ROUTINE, MEANINGLESS PROGRAM. When rightly used these trips are a huge tool. Without proper care, however, even the sharpest of tools becomes dinged and dull. Forgetting the goals of maximum growth, good, and glory will reduce trip leaders to travel agents and participants to sightseers.

SCRATCH DOWN YOUR THOUGHTS

Consider this leader's guide your workbook. In the next chapter you'll find questions to answer as you pick and prepare for a trip. But for now, the biggest questions you can ask yourself and answer are these:

Why do I want to take a group of students on a short-term mission trip? What do I hope it will accomplish?

_____

_____

_____

_____

_____

What do I hope my youth will remember about this trip 10 years from now?

_____

_____

_____

_____

_____

CH. 2

GETTING FROM HERE TO

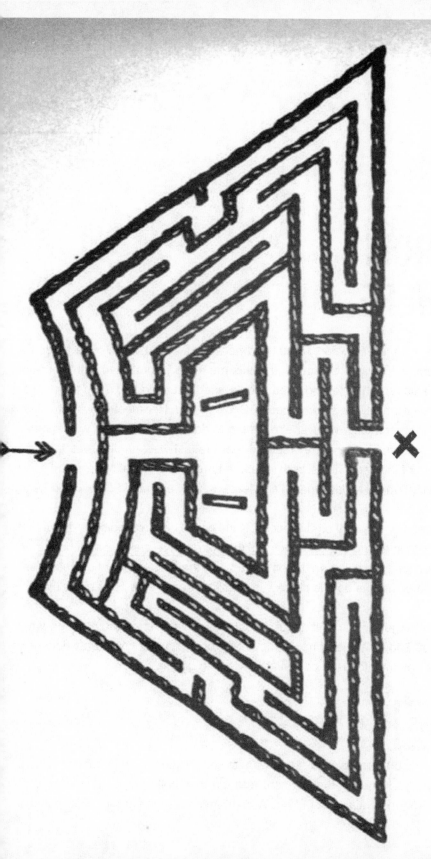

× **THERE**

CH. 2

GETTING FROM
HERE TO THERE

"I realize our church has never done this before," Kathi told her pastor, "but I'd really like to lead a youth mission project this summer. I think it's what God wants me to do." Mom of an eight-year-old too young for the trip she envisioned—and feeling a tad middle-aged to be leading a trip for middle-schoolers and high-schoolers—Kathi still was convinced of God's calling. Her meeting with the pastor secured the backing of the church for "whatever she felt led to do." As she huddled with another adult—a prayer partner and potential leader—they realized that the last week in July was the only summer timeframe that fit both of their schedules. With no spare time for travel, their site would need to be nearby. And as they tallied up likely participants and leaders, they estimated they would need a dozen and a half spots.

After scrutinizing brochures from several organizations, Kathi called her first choice, a group that offered a week-long trip to a site in a tough neighborhood of their large city—a site half an hour from home but a world away. "Well," said the voice on the other end, "on that site we only have an opening left for one week this summer. Let me double check…it looks like we have 19 open spots the last week in July."

Through a process pulled together partly through practical planning—and partly though what looked like the involvement of God—Kathi and her group set off on a trip that crafted a whole new attitude in the youth group, an attitude focused on giving rather than getting.

10 SMART QUESTIONS

If your goal is to participate in short-term missions, you want to know exactly how to get from where you are to where you want to go. Honestly, there's more to a trip than collecting a stack of promotional brochures and videos from potential host groups. A good number of the groups that organize trips for youth groups will provide you with a worthwhile project. But making a trip its most-incredible best for everyone involved—students, parents, trip leaders, hosts, and the people you minister among—depends on you wrapping your brain around some basic issues.

In fact, you need to answer 10 big questions to get from here to there, even before you sign on the dotted line of some host group's contract. When you've adequately answered those questions, you have a lot of your trip figured out. You'll not only know what you'll be doing but why.

Of those 10 questions, there's not a one that you can skip over, even if you're a veteran of many trips. While there's a good chance you'll start with the first question and finish with the last, you won't likely be able to answer the rest sequentially. You'll arrive at answers little by little as you sort through everything.

Answering these questions isn't tough, but they aren't questions that can wait forever. The earlier you can clarify these issues and sign up with a host group, the better your chances of landing the right trip for your group.

As you look through these questions, do whatever fits you: Jot brief notes. Scribble detailed essays. Draw charts and pictures. The answers you generate will be useful to you as your project develops and it comes time to sell the idea to participants, parents, and whoever is in charge at your church or parachurch organization. So have at it—and by the time you're done, you'll know what you're doing and why. And you'll choose a project with confidence.

SMART QUESTION 1: WHAT ARE OUR OPTIONS FOR PLUGGING YOUTH INTO SHORT-TERM MISSIONS?

When your aim is involving your students in short-term missions, your first and only thought might be to join up with one of the well-known organizations that caters to church and parachurch groups looking for group projects.

That's a great idea.

But it's not your only option.

It might not even be the best choice. So before you jump to the conclusion that a group trip is the only way to go, think through these options.

GET YOUR OWN FEET WET. The starting point for engaging your students in short-term missions might not be them. It could be you.

If you've never had any firsthand involvement with a short-term mission project, find a way to plug in now. You'll know far more what short-term missions is about—especially what it can and can't accomplish—if you experience it for yourself. While you might benefit most by experiencing the sensation of getting away from home, you don't have to wave goodbye to your friends, family, and job by signing up for a yearlong stint to the jungle. You could sign up for a short trip for adults. Or you could commit, say, to weekly involvement in a cross-cultural mission project in your own area. There's hardly a place on the planet where that isn't an option.

None of that means you can't or shouldn't take a group just because you've never gone—or that you're necessarily overstepping God's plans just because you have a huge itch to be personally involved in the front lines of missions. But ask yourself this probing question: Is the mission trip I want to do all about me—is it about my desire to get involved—or does God indeed have a bigger plan, one that involves leading a team of youth?

Even if you're a veteran of several trips, you need to ask yourself this question: Is God's right-now call something for me or something for my group? You might feel hugely tugged toward the mission field, but you want to make plans based not solely on what you want or your vision, but on what your group needs.

SEND INDIVIDUAL KIDS. You might be faced with a group so apathetic or burned out that you see only one lone kid ready to plug in. You might have ultramature students looking for more independence or challenge than most group trips provide. Or you might have an impossible time recruiting enough adults to lead your group on a project. Each of those factors and more are reasons to consider finding ways to send individual students on a missions experience. You can point students toward groups geared to individuals. You might dig up opportunities with a denomination or well-known missions boards. Or you might encourage youth to go stay for a summer with a missionary family.

Students who embark alone on a trip can find it utterly transformative. Why? They experience the intensity not only of leaving home but also of leaving familiar faces. They often join up with a project that takes longer, wanders further, and demands more. They get away from everything and can reinvent themselves. And they make friends from all over. (Check with the groups you're interested in: Youth can often sign up and go with a friend or two or more, although the group is likely to frown on friendships if they get in the way of team bonding and teamwork.)

Students who go it alone experience downs along with the ups. Longer trips mean greater expense. Paying for the trip is an individual effort. Returning home can be tough, and they'll surely cry when they say goodbye to their newfound friends. If they arrive home to an unsupportive church or home environment, they can feel no one has experienced what they have—and they might be right. They might even bolt to a church with folks more interested in their experience or with a proven, active missions interest. And all those points raise a concern for you: The positive impact of individual students' trips on your youth group depends on their willingness and ability to communicate what they learned.

Sending individual students doesn't mean sending them unsupported. You can lead a student or a group of students through the preparation and follow-up steps detailed in this book. In fact, you can make it a requirement for receiving financial backing from your church, laying out ahead of time specific expectations on how they'll share what they have learned when they get back. You can stay in touch while they're away. And you can welcome them home and help them process their experience.

STUDENT EXCHANGE PROGRAMS. Anyone working with youth and interested in student missions wields enormous influence in encouraging students to sign up for foreign study programs. While exchange programs aren't purposely set up to be a short-term mission trip, they offer unique opportunities for outreach to classmates, host families, and other program participants. The students who can best hack the life of an exchange student are the same self-starters who take responsibility for their own spiritual growth and ministry at home.

Most programs are open to high school or college students and are best found through students' schools. Legitimate programs are regulated by the Bureau of Educational and Cultural Affairs (ECA) of the U.S. Department of State (http://exchanges.state.gov/education).

With any exchange program, participants can count on six L's: Programs are long-term, usually at least a semester. The focus of most programs isn't missions, but cultural and language learning. Students who leave home for any length of time have losses, things they miss out on because they go. Beware that exchange programs can attract loonies—searching for who knows what—and that going is almost always incredibly lonely (at times). Bottom line: For an adventurous, independent, spiritually mature student, it's a one-of-a-kind load of fun.

Again, you can be part of the preparation of students heading far from home. Because many exchange programs are run by secular organizations, you can help students get serious about locating a church to worship at before they go. And, just as in sending students on a solo mission experience, stay in contact while they're away, be the first to welcome them home, and help them fit into your group when they get back.

GROUP PROJECTS. You can offer a variety of opportunities to match the variety of needs you spot in your students, mixing opportunities for individuals and groups.

Group trips seem easy. Automatic. But they aren't without drawbacks. Because group projects are usually shorter than individual trips, they won't necessarily produce the massive life change of a longer trip. Group trips can lack challenge because they're usually aimed at middle-of-the-pack youth rather than those most gonzo for spiritual growth. Group trips make it easy for you to fall into a rut, do the same thing year after year, and fail to keep the program fresh or to adequately individualize the experience. Group trips—especially to faraway places—can mean raising big money and require the participation of adult leaders, which can skewer a project when leaders run scarce.

Even with those potential drawbacks, however, a group project can be wildly beneficial to your group. For starters it lets you open the experience of short-term missions to many more students in your youth group than a select few. Perhaps you want more reasons to pursue a group project. Read on.

+ Students are more likely to participate because they can face the challenges of a project along with familiar friends and leaders.

+ Students will join up because they trust you, even if they don't comprehend every detail of what they'll be doing or where they'll be going.

+ Parents feel better sending their kids with known leaders, provided you have a track record of reliability.

+ You can personally shape what your students do and learn.

+ Group trips mobilize combined power to accomplish tasks.

+ Your group bonds and grows in community and unity in ways impossible to duplicate by sending individuals.

+ When you are a part of the actual trip (a likely possibility), you can wrap the trip into an integrated program that includes preparation and follow-up.

SETTING OFF ON YOUR OWN

IF YOU'VE SETTLED ON A GROUP TRIP AS YOUR MAIN CHOICE, YOU'VE MAYBE CONSIDERED ROLLING YOUR OWN MISSION TRIP—PLANNING THE DETAILS FROM START TO FINISH, SKIPPING INVOLVEMENT WITH A HOST GROUP WHO CAN OFFER A VARIETY OF SERVICES TO FACILITATE YOUR TRIP.

DON'T GO THERE.

AT THE VERY LEAST YOU NEED LOCAL CONNECTIONS TO CREATE A WORTHWHILE TRIP. AT WORST YOU MIGHT WIND UP ON A NIGHTMARISH PROJECT—LIKE THE COLLEGE GROUP WITH NO YOUTH WORK OR CAMPING EXPERIENCE WHO INSERTED THEMSELVES INTO AN EX-SOVIET REPUBLIC AS THE SOLE ORGANIZERS AND LEADERS OF A CAMP FOR SEVERAL HUNDRED NATIONAL YOUTH. CAN YOU PICTURE THE CHAOS?

UNTIL YOU HAVE THE EXPERIENCE YOU NEED TO BOLDLY GO YOUR OWN WAY—AFTER MULTIPLE TRIPS—YOUR BEST OPTION IS TO SEEK A HOST GROUP THAT COVERS THE GROUNDWORK FOR YOU. FOR THE PURPOSES OF THIS BOOK, WE'LL ASSUME YOU'RE SIGNING UP WITH AN EXPERIENCED HOST.

Right now you've got a chicken-and-egg choice: You want to go with the right group, but you want the right project. You'll need to get a feel for the host group and the specifics on the trips they provide. But for now, back up to some big questions:

What's driving your desire to undertake a trip now? Who wants it? Why?

_____

_____

_____

_____

_____

Would it be better for our group to send individual students or to pursue a group project? Reasons?

_____

_____

_____

_____

_____

Why rule out other options?

_____

_____

_____

_____

SMART QUESTION 2: WHAT DO WE WANT TO DO AND EXPERIENCE?

There's no so such thing as a one-size-fits-all missions experience. Short-term mission projects can take you from a mountain wilderness to the desert to the world's largest urban settings. You can work in your own backyard or serve almost anywhere in the Americas, Europe, Asia, Australia, or Africa. You can go where Christ is unknown or barely known—or serve closer to home where you'll discover the needs are still great. You can rough it or live in relative comfort.

Once you've arrived onsite, you can do almost any imaginable activity, supporting existing missionaries, serving national Christians, or directly working with non-Christians. You can serve quietly in the background or attract positive attention to create opportunities to overtly share your faith. Check out the variety of activities youth can take on during short-term missions:

building churches	rehabbing houses	leading evangelistic Bible studies
ministering through sports	helping start churches	cooking
teaching English	sharing testimonies	leading Vacation Bible Schools
cleaning	leading worship services	camping
biking	performing with puppets	constructing schools
demolishing buildings	motor biking	providing childcare
tutoring	ministering in nursing homes	clowning
digging	visiting juvenile lock-ups	putting on plays and sketches
witnessing in the streets	painting murals	distributing tracts
assisting senior citizens	weeding	praying
counseling	making crafts	dancing
developing friendships	encouraging local believers	feeding the hungry
handing out Bibles	performing mime	playing music
working in an orphanage	helping in health clinics	hiking
painting	ministering in prisons	

The Bible coaches us to use the gifts we have (1 Peter 4:10), so settling on the type of experience that best fits your youth is hugely important. While it's difficult to lump trips into cut-and-dried categories, it's common to make a basic distinction between so-called work projects and evangelistic projects. But even swinging hammers or caring for the elderly—when done for our maximum growth, others' maximum good, and God's maximum glory—is evangelistic at some level. It's better to think in terms of some trips highlighting witness by deeds—doing hands-on work—and others majoring on witness by words, engaging in some form of verbal witness. Many deliberately do both.

In what setting would we be most effective? Is there a location we prefer? What living conditions would we enjoy—or be able to cope with?

_____

_____

_____

_____

Whom do we want to work with? Is there a particular age group or population of people we would like to serve?

_____

_____

_____

_____

What interests does our group have? What skills can we offer? Is there a ministry we do here and now that we can do somewhere else? Who—in our congregation or from an outside group—can teach us a skill to equip us for a project? Or what have we dreamed of doing?

_____

_____

_____

_____

SMART QUESTION 3: WHAT'S THE BEST TIMING FOR A TRIP?

Obviously you can't just decide where to go; you also need to know when. While most student trips take place during summer vacation, some host groups offer projects over Christmas and Easter breaks.

Like planning for any other extended event, sooner or later you'll run into scheduling conflicts. Even if you're planning your trip for the wide expanse of summer, you'll obviously want to check calendars for possible conflicts with school calendars, sports tournaments, community events, and church programs. You might create a foul mood, for instance, if you take away a bunch of key youth and adult volunteers the week of your own church's vacation Bible school. And it doesn't do much good to go head-to-head with existing youth programs like camps or community events like the zucchini festival or state fair.

Part of the when question is also asking how long a trip you want to undertake. Short trips are like running hard and fast in a sprint. Longer trips develop endurance. While it might sound appealing to flee the country for a month or more, your potential adult staff might not share your enthusiasm. Even though adventurous high school students may like the idea of longer trips, summer jobs reduce their availability. Since various host groups offer projects that last from a weekend to a week to the bulk of a summer, start your brainstorming by considering all your options.

One last consideration regarding the when of your trip is whether you have enough time to pull off a trip. You know your own people, setting, and organizational abilities—and whether approval of a trip hinges on clearing several church committees. Heads up: Some host groups start sign-ups for summer trips as soon as their current summer trips are completed. First dibs often go to groups returning to the same time slot and location.

How long a trip do we want to take? Why?

_____

_____

_____

When exactly do we anticipate taking a trip? What reasons do we have to go then? Do we have adequate time to pull the trip together?

_____

_____

_____

_____

What conflicts with school, sports, community, and church programs exist if we choose those dates? Who might get left behind?

_____

_____

_____

_____

SMART QUESTION 4: WHO ARE WE AIMING TO TAKE?

Even though deciding where you'd like to go and what chunk of time you need to block out on a calendar is incredibly important, you have bigger questions to answer. After all, you're not planning a trip for the sake of a trip. You're aiming to impact real youth.

So whom do you plan to take?

You probably don't have the option to handpick your student participants, even if you wanted to. Think about the goofballs God recruited and trained for outreach: Nathanael the earnest seeker of truth. Matthew the tax collector. Peter the fisherman. Thomas the doubter. Simon the political fanatic. Even Judas the betrayer. The Bible sometimes paints this motley crew as spiritually dense. And yet Jesus poured his efforts into them.

As you think about students you want to engage in a mission project, keep in mind that the ones most interested in giving up their time to serve might not be the most popular, vocal, or outgoing kids. They might be quiet, committed kids scared off by boisterous crowds—kids who want to participate in missions, but kids you might hardly have seen at your youth group meetings. If you're lucky, you won't just attract the spiritually best and brightest. You'll pull students from the fringe.

You might think it's absolutely backward to take students struggling in their faith. You might aim to raise the bar incredibly high for students participating in mission events. You might be tempted to scare off the uncommitted by reams of application requirements and months of regimented preparation.

Think again. Some projects do necessitate spiritual maturity. Students can't lead others into

God's new birth if they themselves are spiritually dead. But even Jesus sent out his disciples to communicate the good news of the kingdom when they possessed a less-than-perfect understanding of him. Some deed-oriented projects can be outreaches to the participants themselves. You'll find a huge difference in the spiritual maturity required for street evangelism versus scraping paint.

Jesus drew people to God by treating the marginalized with significance. Entrusting teens with the job of helping others is an enormous way you can wrap them in God's love by communicating significance.

A few final thoughts on who to take.

+ While a host group will likely tell you what ages your students should be, you still need to decide ahead of time your upper and lower age limits for participants.

The target age of your group might already be decided by your youth group structure. You might already know you need a trip for high schoolers—or for middle schoolers. If you usually keep those age groups separated, you might have a mob of mad students if you take them on a trip together—putting them in an environment where they bond—only to split them up again back home. Still, if you can find a workable way to mix ages, you get the bonus of older students modeling for younger ones or upstart younger students setting the pace for older slackers.

+ A growing number of host groups tailor trips for families, even those with young children. While planning and running a family-oriented trip probably won't change your workload preparing for the trip, you're guaranteed to have parents involved on site and you're relieved of a huge supervisory and disciplinary role. If you're up for an adventure, ponder these questions: Why take parents and siblings? Why not?

CHOOSING PARTICIPANTS

YOU MIGHT ACHE TO PLAN AN ADVANCED TRIP FOR THE SPIRITUALLY MATURE. BUT YOUR REAL CHALLENGE IS TO OPEN UP OPPORTUNITIES FOR ALL YOUR KIDS. YOU WANT ALL YOUTH TO UNDERSTAND THAT SERVICE IS AN EVERYDAY PART OF THE NORMAL CHRISTIAN LIFE. YOU WANT TO GIVE ALL STUDENTS A CHANCE TO RISE TO THE OCCASION. AND THE LAST THING YOU WANT TO DO IS CREATE A SENSE THAT MISSIONS IS A JOB RESERVED FOR THE SPIRITUAL ELITE.

YOUR BEST ROUTE MIGHT BE TO LET YOUTH SELF-SELECT, THAT IS, TO DECIDE FOR THEMSELVES WHETHER THEY'RE UP FOR A PARTICULAR TRIP. YOU CAN DO THAT BY LAYING OUT THE BENEFITS AND COSTS OF THE PROJECT, MIXED WITH A HUGE DOSE OF ENCOURAGEMENT THAT THEY'RE CAPABLE OF MEETING THE CHALLENGE. AND FOR ALL BUT THE SHORTEST, MOST ENTRY-LEVEL PROJECTS, YOU CAN REQUIRE STUDENTS TO GO THROUGH A MODEST APPLICATION PROCESS.

REQUIRING AN APPLICATION FROM YOUR STUDENTS—RATHER THAN SIMPLY HAVING SIGN-UPS— CAN HELP THEM SELF-SELECT BY FORCING A CONSCIOUS, THOUGHTFUL CHOICE ABOUT TAKING PART IN THE TRIP. YOUR GOAL IS TO PROD YOUTH TO PONDER AND BRIEFLY ANSWER QUESTIONS SUCH AS THESE:

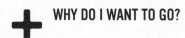 WHY DO I WANT TO GO?

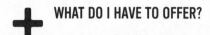 WHAT DO I HAVE TO OFFER?

 WHAT HAVE I BEEN DOING TO PREPARE ME FOR THIS PROJECT?

A REASONABLE DEADLINE SETS A SERIOUS TONE AND GETS COMMITMENT ON PAPER, NOT LETTING STUDENTS SLIDE THROUGH MONTHS OF "I'M THINKING ABOUT IT."

AN APPLICATION MAKES SERVICE A PRIVILEGE, A HOT COMMODITY. THE GOAL IS TO INCLUDE STUDENTS, NOT EXCLUDE. YET A CARELESSLY COMPLETED APPLICATION ALSO GIVES YOU CONCRETE INFORMATION AND A KIND WAY TO SAY, "I'M NOT SURE THIS IS THE BEST FIT FOR YOU. HERE'S A DIFFERENT OPPORTUNITY I WANT YOU TO THINK ABOUT."

IF YOU FIND A MOB OF STUDENTS MISMATCHING THEMSELVES FOR A PARTICULAR TRIP, YOU'RE EITHER PUSHING TOO HARD TO GET KIDS TO APPLY OR YOU'RE HIGHLIGHTING THE BENEFITS OF THE TRIP AND NEGLECTING THE COSTS.

ARE YOU PLANNING A TRIP FOR FIRST-TIMERS? OR ARE YOU THINKING OF A TRIP FOR THE SPIRITUALLY MATURE? FEEL GOOD ABOUT STARTING SMALL AND EASY WITH A TRIP ACCESSIBLE TO EVERYBODY. THEN, IF YOU FIND KIDS WHO CRAVE MORE, DEVELOP AN ADVANCED TRIP. MAKE OLDER STUDENTS ASSISTANT LEADERS OR TEEN HELPERS ON YOUR BEGINNER TRIP. OR SEND A SELECT FEW KIDS ON INDIVIDUAL TRIPS. BUT MAKE MISSIONS AN OPPORTUNITY FOR EVERYONE.

How many students can we accommodate on a trip—especially if this is our first trip?

_____

What type of student will benefit from this trip? Who specifically do I see as candidates?

_____

_____

Who won't fit? What age group or type of student are we leaving out? What alternative opportunities can we provide for those who don't go?

_____

_____

_____

How do we want to recruit? Will we use applications—and how will we use them?

_____

_____

SMART QUESTION 5: WHO CAN HELP ME UNDERTAKE THIS TRIP?

Chapters 3 and 4 describe jobs you'll need help with. You need people to assist with prep work. You need adults to actually go on the trip. And what you're looking for is a team that together possesses the crucial qualities needed by a good short-term mission trip leader.

It isn't rocket science to give your group the kind of world-changing missions experience that aims for maximum growth, maximum good, and maximum glory. But here's one sure truth: No rocket can fly if someone doesn't pump in the gas. At this moment in time, that gas-pumper seems to be you! Whether you're a seasoned youth worker, a newbie volunteer, or a reluctant draftee, God has a place for you in his plan to teach youth and reach the world.

Mission trips need quality leadership. And the first quality necessary to lead is availability. It's simply the desire to clear your schedule and expend energy to get involved with what God wants to do in and through a group of teens. Yet leadership is also about ability. Short-term mission trip chaperones need a few basic qualities:

+ A LOVE FOR YOUTH. That seems obvious—until you meet a batch of adults who go because they feel guilty, because their child is going, because they want to prey on kids, et cetera.

+ A SENSE OF ADVENTURE. Serving always pulls us out of our comfortable home turf and our familiar environments. Leaders don't get to whine about tough living conditions or hard work.

+ AN ABILITY TO SUPERVISE TASKS TO COMPLETION. Whether you're hanging doors or evangelizing door to door, leaders need to know how to pace tasks and keep work moving.

+ MOTIVATIONAL GIFTS. Promising to dye your hair green won't pay off like talking to the kids about the unique satisfaction they'll feel from fixing a blind lady's house.

IT ISN'T YOUR JOB TO SELL THE IDEA OF SHORT-TERM MISSIONS TO HUGE NUMBERS OF STUDENTS. WHAT'S IMPORTANT AT THE START IS LEADING BY EXAMPLE—AND BEGINNING WITH A FEW YOUTH WHO ALREADY GET IT OR AT LEAST HAVE GLIMPSED THE COOLNESS OF SERVING GOD.

+ SKILL AT EXPLAINING WHAT YOU'RE DOING. Jesus didn't just send his disciples off. He prepared them beforehand and processed the experience with them afterward. A leader's ability to explain the Christian motivation behind even practical tasks is what makes a mission trip different from volunteer work students do for Scouts or public schools.

+ COMMITMENT TO ONGOING SERVICE. A leader needs to connect the project to the rest of the youth program and to develop continuing opportunities for youth to serve. Chapters 11 and 12 of this guide will give you follow-up ideas to help your youth bring the trip home.

Does that list of gifts sound absolutely unreasonable? Yes. Unless you're Jesus, you don't have all of them. That's why you recruit multiple leaders. And that means one adult involved needs the ability to pull together a team of adults.

Banish the thought of ever doing a mission project solo. Not even if you're leading a half dozen kids on a day trip. You can't do a project alone. Why? For starters, your church or parachurch organization should have policies that ensure the safety of kids and limit the church's liability by having at least two adults present at any youth event. But there's more. A mixed group of guys and girls needs at least one male leader and one female leader. If you ever run into trouble, you need an adult to go for help while another stays with the youth in need. Besides, you need another adult to tell you when you have lunch leftovers stuck in your teeth or when the youth have taped a "kick me" sign to your back.

And here's the biggie: Because no one person has all the gifts, energy, and personality to pull off a project all by her lonesome, you'll have a better trip with multiple leaders.

No one person is adequate as a leader for a trip. Your varied students will bond with leaders who vary in skills, temperament, and leadership style. And you need to tap into the wisdom and enthusiasm located in different members of the body of Christ. If you're a 19-year-old, part-time, first-job youth director, that's fantastic. You can run circles around the old folk. But you might balance yourself out with a parent trusted by other parents in the church. If you're a visionary older adult who hasn't chaperoned a youth trip in a decade, find a younger coleader still eager to stay up late, eat cruddy food, and sleep on the floor.

One last tip to keep in mind as you recruit adult leaders: The longer your trip…the more youth you take…the further from civilization you wander…the handier it is to bring along a medical professional—a nurse, emergency medical technician, physician's assistant, or doctor—who can take charge of sick or injured students.

How much help—and what kind of help—can we reasonably expect from people as we assemble everything needed for the trip? What do we expect from each of these key groups?

Students

_____

_____

Parents

_____

_____

Pastor and church board

_____

_____

Other adults in the church

_____

_____

Our host group

_____

_____

Which adults might help plan and lead this trip?

_____

_____

Who do I—the point person for the trip—need to balance my skills, temperament, age, gender, et cetera?

_____

_____

Are we ready to make a commitment to taking a mission trip? Do we as leaders have any reservations about the trip that will get in the way of its effectiveness?

_____

_____

SMART QUESTION 6: WHO COULD OUR GROUP GO WITH?

Could. That's a word meant to expand your choices. Smart Question 7 will help you narrow your choice to the group you should go with.

If you're a recent arrival on the youth-leading scene at your church, you might have inherited a tradition of working with a particular host group--or even a signed contract for an upcoming trip. Think hard before you undo something that's already been done—and don't undo it. If you're the one who hasn't gone with the group while the kids have, you can create a disaster by unraveling the relationship. Unless you have solid evidence it's been unsafe, immoral, or totally defective, do their trip—at least once. Have a look before you make drastic changes.

If you're completely free to look for a host group, the groups you might already know and love are great places to start. You might already be aware of programs that give you the chance to serve far away or in a city or rural area nearby. Some might be run by your church, denomination, or association. Others may be groups your church works with often. Going with one of those organizations means you'll be aware of whom you're going with, what you'll be doing, and what the experience will be like for students and adults.

But you might not realize the variety of other sources you have nearby for locating other potential host groups. You can broaden your choices by checking with—

 Your church's ministries or committees focused on outreach, social justice, evangelism, or missions. Whatever label these people wear in your setting, you probably have people tapped into local, national, or international outreaches where you could serve.

Your pastor

Your denomination or like-minded churches

Neighboring churches

Missionaries supported by your church and their sending agencies

You aren't looking for hearsay. You want first-hand recommendations. But what if you don't have immediate information on a group or have any of those leads? Go to www.youthspecialties.com/central and click on Missions Information in the drop-down menu to link to an array of groups currently offering trips.

See Smart Question 7 for ideas about how to evaluate potential host groups.

What obligations do we have to maintain current programs or the organization our group has used in the past? Why would we use that group? What reasons do we have to change?

_____

_____

_____

_____

Who can I ask for information on short-term mission projects? Whom do they suggest? My best-guess list of host groups to investigate is...

_____

_____

_____

SMART QUESTION 7: HOW DO WE PICK THE RIGHT GROUP — AND THE RIGHT TRIP?

You're expecting the staff of a host group to provide you with a good-fitting, spiritually significant trip. You're trusting them with your time, energy, and money, not to mention your group's health and safety. So who are these people? If you take time to look around, you'll find a mind-boggling array of host organizations and trip offerings.

The cost of trips runs from expensive to surprisingly reasonable. Some groups have a strong theological or denominational slant or cater to groups only within their associations. A group might expect a level of spiritual maturity you can't claim for your teens or an evangelistic boldness you don't feel comfortable with. Some organization hosts have hundreds of kids from dozens of churches on a single site. Others craft a trip just for you. Some lead you and your youth through a tightly supervised experience. Others make arrangements on your behalf but let you get your group to a site and run your own show—not a task for first-timers.

While you might be tempted to sign up with the group supplying the slickest brochure or promo video, it pays to do your homework—to ask at least as many questions as you do when you check your dog into a kennel. It would be tough to ask every potential group all these questions, but look for answers to these questions when you peruse brochures and Web sites. Then get on the phone or face-to-face for details when you're ready to narrow your choice to a group or two.

When it's time to ask these questions, get paper and a pen ready and jot yourself some notes. Don't listen just for information but for cooperation—an attitude of helpfulness and teamwork that makes a trip successful.

BACKGROUND

+ Tell me about your ministry. How long has your organization been around? Who is in charge? How many youth have you taken on trips?

+ What kinds of trips do you offer? What are the tasks we might do and the locations we could go to?

+ What kind of youth does your group cater to? What level of spiritual maturity or missions experience to you expect?

+ What makes you different from other short-term mission groups?

+ Do you have a written statement of faith? What kinds of churches do you work with?

+ Whom can I talk to who has used your group before?

THE STAFF

+ How many staff members will be on site? What's their training? Who are they?

+ Who from your staff will be with us? What will they do exactly?

+ Do you do Bible teaching during the trip? Who does it? What's the theme?

+ Do you have anyone on site with medical or first-aid training?

THE EXPERIENCE

+ What's the typical daily schedule? What do we do in the mornings? How long is the work day? What do we do in the evenings?

+ How many students will serve at our site?

+ Would our group be the only one at the site or would we serve with students from other churches?

+ What are the living conditions like?

+ What rules do you expect students to follow?

+ What kind of preparation do you expect of the participants? What do you do to help with that?

+ What do you to do to help the kids take their trip home?

+ Will our youth get split up onto teams with students from other churches? If so, will they always be paired with another student from our church? Will each of our youth work with at least one of the adults from our church?

YOUR ROLE

+ What role do our adult leaders take?

+ How many adults do you require for our group—the required student/leader ratio?

+ What do we need to administrate properly?

+ What does it cost?

+ When are reservations and registration forms due?

+ When are payments due?

+ Can you provide us with ideas for fundraising?

THE SITE

+ What safety issues at this site should we be aware of?

+ What do students need to do to stay healthy in the site environment? Any special concerns?

+ What cross-cultural issues might we encounter at this site?

+ What are sleeping, bathroom, and shower facilities like?

+ What sightseeing or recreational activities are available?

BIG MISSIONS QUESTIONS

+ What do you honestly expect us to accomplish?

+ How do you anticipate our students will grow?

+ How will we be involved with local Christians?

+ What do the people at the project site think about God? About us? About our task?

+ How will our work be followed up after we leave?

There's one big area of concern that's tough to nail down before you arrive on site: the quality of the host staff who work with your youth. You'll almost always meet some incredibly great staff; you might encounter others who can unravel your trip. That's information to share honestly with a site supervisor or host organization—and to learn from.

SMART QUESTION 8: HOW ARE WE GOING TO ENGAGE PARENTS IN THE VISION FOR THIS TRIP?

Parents?

In the grand scheme of youth ministry, lots of youth workers see parents as second only to supervising pastors as gigantic speed bumps they need to clear to get to "real" youth ministry. They resent anyone who questions their skills or who tests their maturity.

But you can dare to think differently: Parents are part of your ministry, as coworkers, supporters, and beneficiaries of a ministry done well. The same is true of senior pastors and other church leadership. If you have a fundamental distrust of parents and their pals, it can be hard to understand the depth to which they don't look kindly on youth leaders who use, lose, or abuse kids. And if you're contemplating a trip to someplace distant or dangerous, you might be asking for more trust than ever before. Parents were responsible to teach your students to cross the street solo. So don't be surprised if they break a sweat when you tell them you want to crisscross the globe. Their little babies might need a passport—not to mention some shots they didn't get when they were newborns.

And here's where reality hits the fan: If you don't adequately explain your plans to parents and the church leadership, you won't be taking the trip you're thinking so hard about.

+ Parents aren't looking for snow jobs. Not even a sell job. They want an objective view of what you plan to do—including what it will cost, what the trip will accomplish in their youth, and exactly how you will need them to help. They want a realistic presentation of the risks.

+ The response you'll get to your plans is guaranteed to be mixed. Some parents are thrilled out of their minds. Others think you are out of your mind. A few parents think their kids couldn't possibly be capable of handling the trip you're describing. (Maybe they're right, but there's only one way to find out.) Some families have unbreakable previous commitments. Others aren't ready to send their kids to someplace perceived as out of the way or dangerous. If you offer a trip for middle schoolers, you might be surprised how many haven't been away from home for even a week and don't feel comfortable making a mission project the first plunge.

You can model respect and cooperation for your students by treating parents' concerns seriously. After all, they want what's best for their children. Admittedly, some need to be gently educated that their children's involvement in God's plan for the world is part of "best."

One key thought some need to hear is that your goal isn't to force their kids to become career missionaries—your goal is to help students explore their places in God's plan, uncover their giftedness, and catch a glimpse of God's love in the world. You're aiming to apprentice students in the faith and make service a normal part of the Christian life. A call to missions—which can take a lot of evidence to discern—is between each of the students and God.

✝ If you know why you're undertaking this trip and have quizzed your hosting group on the issues raised under Smart Question 7, you'll be prepared to answer when parents start asking questions, but here are a couple key questions to ask yourself about engaging parents:

What do I need to do to get parents on board with this project? Which key parents will make or break this trip?

_____

_____

_____

_____

What objections do I anticipate parents will raise?

_____

_____

_____

How would I like parents to help?

_____

_____

_____

SMART QUESTION 9: HOW DO I MAKE THIS WORK WITHIN MY CHURCH OR ORGANIZATION?

Even if you aren't a paid youth staffer at a church or parachurch group, you can't ignore the problem of making a trip work within your organizational setting. If you announce a trip to students before you chat with the proper leader types, you're begging for trouble in all but the most laid-back groups.

Identify the key decision makers whose approval you need to garner—the youth board, the senior pastor, the church council from whom all budgetary blessings flow and through whom all big decisions pass. Most battles aren't over whether to do a mission trip but what the key details are: How far? How long? At what cost?

Leaders in organizational hierarchies likely have an opinion on fundraising. Scheduling. Expenses. Who's in charge. Potential safety issues that expose the group to lawsuits. They'll want to know what host group you want to work with and why—and you might discover some leaders have an agenda about whom they think you should work with.

Inability to provide any vital bits of information will skewer your trip.

While some leaders want to be informed every step of the way, almost all will want to meet with you at the start and finish of your planning. Go to them with "This is what I'm thinking," as well as "This is what I think we should do," when you have all but made a decision.

How do we make this trip work within our system? Whose backing do we need to move forward for formal approval?

_____

_____

_____

Whose formal approval do we need? In what areas will these people want to sign off?

_____

_____

_____

ANSWERING OBJECTIONS TO SHORT-TERM MISSIONS

WHEN YOU PROPOSE A TRIP, YOU COULD RUN INTO DEEPER RESISTANCE THAN YOU EVER IMAGINED. YOU AND YOUR YOUTH MIGHT DREAM OF HEADING TO THE ENDS OF THE PLANET TO TELL PEOPLE ABOUT CHRIST THROUGH WORDS AND ACTIONS. BUT NOT EVERYONE THINKS THAT WAY. SOME CHRISTIANS HEAR "SHORT-TERM MISSIONS" AND SHUDDER. THEY HAVE A LONG LIST OF OBJECTIONS WHY YOUTH AND OTHER SHORT-TERMERS HAVE NO PLACE IN MISSIONS.

+ YOU JUST SAY GO.   + THEY JUST SAY NO.

YOU PROBABLY WON'T BE ABLE TO CHANGE THE MINDS OF PEOPLE DEAD SET AGAINST STUDENT INVOLVEMENT IN MISSIONS. BUT YOU'LL HAVE AN ADVANTAGE IF YOU'RE AWARE OF THE OBJECTIONS—AND HAVE RESPONSES TO THEM.

+ *STUDENTS AREN'T REAL MISSIONARIES.* YOUTH WON'T MATCH THE MATURITY OF ADULT MISSIONARIES TRAINED TO THE HILT AND SIGNED UP FOR LIFE. THEY MIGHT NOT FULLY BE AWARE OF THE SACRIFICES MADE BY MISSIONARIES OF THE PAST—LIKE THE FOLKS WHO STOOD ON THE DECKS OF SHIPS AND WAVED AS THEY SAILED OFF, KNOWING THEY WERE LEAVING HOME TO FACE CERTAIN DEATH IN THE AMERICAS OR AFRICA OR ASIA. BUT GOD HAS GIVEN ALL OF US THE TASK OF SPREADING THE GOOD NEWS. EVEN THE FRESHEST OF BELIEVERS CAN BE HIS "AMBAS-SADORS, AS THOUGH GOD WERE MAKING HIS APPEAL THROUGH US" (2 CORINTHIANS 5:17-20).

HALF OF YOUR SOLUTION IS TO CRAFT A TRIP THAT ISN'T JUST SIGHTSEEING BUT SACRIFICIAL- AND SERVICE-ORIENTED. THE OTHER HALF IS TO HAVE A PLAN TO HELP RETURNING STUDENTS FIGURE OUT HOW TO GET INVOLVED IN MISSIONS IN A LONG-TERM WAY. BEING YOUNG DOESN'T MEAN A TEEN CAN'T DO REAL MINISTRY.

+ *STUDENTS DON'T UNDERSTAND THE CULTURE.* WAVING THE WRONG WAY IN ANOTHER CULTURE MIGHT MEAN YOU WANT TO MAKE TROUBLE—OR MAKE OUT. ACCEPTING THE WRONG DINNER INVITATION MAY MEAN YOU JUST SAID YES TO GETTING ENGAGED. CULTURE CAN BE A PUZZLE. BUT ANY SMART LONG-TERM HOST YOU WORK WITH CAN TELL YOU THE TOP 10 WAYS TO BE RUDE OR OFFENSIVE IN A PARTICULAR CULTURE AND HOW TO AVOID THEM.

THIS PROTEST IS LOSING ITS PUNCH IN OUR SHRINKING WORLD. CENTRAL ASIA GETS BETTER CABLE STATION THAN WE DO, AND OUR STUDENTS ARE GROWING UP IN A GLOBAL YOUTH CULTURE. EVEN SUBURBAN AMERICA ISN'T MONOCHROMATIC—A PLACE WHERE EVERYONE LOOKS AND ACTS AND BELIEVES THE SAME. STUDENTS ARE FORCED TO PRACTICE CULTURAL SENSITIVITY EVERY TIME THEY GO TO SCHOOL.

+ *STUDENTS COST TOO MUCH MONEY.* GOING FOR A FEW WEEKS TO A FAR-OFF PLACE DOES COST THOUSANDS OF DOLLARS. THE MONEY SPENT TO SEND A STUDENT FOR A SUMMER MIGHT SUPPORT SEVERAL LOCAL WORKERS FOR A YEAR.

YOU DO HAVE TO QUESTION THE SENSE OF FLYING TO MOUNT EVEREST FOR A WEEK OR A WEEKEND. MOST OF THE COST IS AIRFARE, SO A LONG-DISTANCE TRIP BECOMES COST-EFFECTIVE ONLY WHEN YOU STAY A WHILE. AND WHEREVER YOU GO, PEOPLE RIGHTLY EXPECT YOU TO WORK—NOT GOOF OFF.

BUT CHEW ON THIS. SUPPOSE THE ADULTS AT CHURCH SPEND $3000 TO SEND A STUDENT SOMEWHERE THIS SUMMER.

POSSIBILITY 1: THAT STUDENT IS HOOKED AND GOD'S CAUSE GAINS A CAREER MISSIONARY.

POSSIBILITY 2: THAT STUDENT NEVER TAKES PART IN ANOTHER MISSION TRIP, BUT UNDERSTANDS THE CAUSE OF MISSIONS. THE MONEY INVESTED IN THAT STUDENT IS PAID BACK MANY TIMES THROUGH THE MONEY, TIME, AND ENERGY HE POURS BACK INTO GOD'S CAUSE OVER A LIFETIME.

+ *STUDENTS WILL ENCOUNTER DANGER THEY WON'T BE ABLE TO HANDLE.* MANY SHORT-TERM TRIPS TAKE KIDS OUT OF THEIR COMFORT ZONE. THEY GO TO STRANGE PLACES. THEY SEE DRUG DEALERS, HUNGER, DISEASE, DRUNKENNESS, SPIRITUAL DARKNESS. IT CAN BE PHYSICALLY AND EMOTIONALLY ROUGH.

DON'T BE STUPID. KEEP YOUR YOUTH OUT OF PLACES WHERE MISSIONARIES RISK BEING KIDNAPPED AND KILLED. BUT YOU CAN FEND OFF UNFOUNDED FEARS BY ADDRESSING LEGITIMATE CONCERNS.

+ *STUDENTS GET IN THE WAY OF REAL MISSIONARIES.* THEY DO IF THEY TAKE OFF ON A PROJECT UNPREPARED AND UNCOACHED. BUT IF YOU GO WITH A WELL-SEASONED HOST AND DO WHAT THEY TELL YOU, NOT ONLY WILL STUDENTS NOT GET IN THE WAY, BUT THEY'LL ALSO ACCOMPLISH TASKS THAT THE CAREER MISSIONARIES CAN'T. YOUR TEAM CAN BRING THE ENERGY AND VISIBILITY THEY NEED, FOR EXAMPLE, BY TEACHING A VACATION BIBLE SCHOOL, PUTTING TOGETHER A TEAM OF BASKETBALL PLAYERS THAT CAN ATTRACT SOME POSITIVE ATTENTION, OR PERFORMING STREET DRAMAS.

SMART QUESTION 10: HOW MUCH WILL THIS COST?

Here's a point that might be no big deal—or a whopper that makes or breaks your trip. The next chapter details ways you can finance your trip. For now, think through how much you'll need to spend to accomplish what you want to do. Do the math and figure out the cost-per-youth.

✚ On top of what a host group charges you per student and per adult leader, you have overhead. While some of your trip's costs might be billed against the youth group's overall budget, you might need to build some expenses into the price paid by each student.

✚ What are your likely expenses? You'll need money on the front end for publicity and preparation materials. You might elect to make a pretrip visit to your site. During the trip you'll need funds for transportation to your site and possibly on site—for instance, from your housing to wherever you do your project. Depending on how your project is structured or how long you'll be on the road, you might need to figure in food, lodging, work supplies, teaching or evangelistic supplies, film, and film developing.

Double check that your vehicle insurance, for example, covers you where you're going. You'll also need to calculate out-of-pocket expenses you expect students to cover—recreation, shopping, snacks, and meals on the trip. And you'll want some emergency cash on hand—a slush fund for unforeseen expenses.

 Use the **Cost Worksheet** on page 52 to figure the costs of your trip.

 If you absolutely have to cut costs but don't want to sacrifice the goals of the project, think through these large items:
✚ Should we do a trip that is local or closer to home?
✚ Should we go for a shorter period of time?
✚ Should we find no-cost lodging while traveling to and from the site?

Does this project seem cost efficient? Can we defend this cost to students, parents, and the church?

_____

_____

_____

If you noodle the numbers and aren't satisfied, skip ahead to **Paying for Your Trip** (page 71). You'll find advice on getting the funds you need to get from here to there—including some tips that may help you rethink the trip you've picked.

PUTTING IT ALL TOGETHER

Your trip is so much more than signing up and showing up. Thinking through all the details can make your brain ache, but, if you've thought through these issues, you're well on your way to a trip that causes growth in your youth, does good to other people, and brings glory to God. You're may even be ready to hook up with a host group and sign on the dotted line of a trip contract.

Summarize what you've learned—and you'll be ready to gather students to the cause.

Where are we going to go—when, with whom, to do what?

_____

_____

_____

_____

Why did we pick *this* trip? Give three good reasons.

_____

_____

_____

_____

_____

_____

COST WORKSHEET

Publicity costs $ _____

Preparation materials $ _____

Pre-trip visit $ _____

Transportation (to site) $ _____

Transportation (on site) $ _____

Work supplies $ _____

Teaching or evangelistic supplies $ _____

Film and developing $ _____

Emergency cash $ _____

Additional Insurance $ _____

Food   ($ _____ per student per day
          X _____ days X _____ students =) $ _____

Lodging ($ _____ per student per day
          X _____ days X _____ students =) $ _____

Subsidizing cost of adult leaders $ _____

TOTAL $ _____

Total divided by number of students
equals cost per student: $ _____
What remaining expenses will students need to cover out of pocket
(recreation, shopping, snacks, meals while traveling)?

GRAND TOTAL COST PER STUDENT: $ _____

Are there costs we can cut without sacrificing the goals of the project?
Some large items to think through:

+ Should we do a trip that is local or within a couple hours of home?

+ Should we go for a shorter period of time?

+ Should we find no-cost lodging while traveling to and from the site?

CH. 3

HEX CAP SCREWS

HEX BOLTS

CARRIAGE BOLTS

RIBBED NECK

HEX LAG SCREWS

SQUARE LAG SCREWS

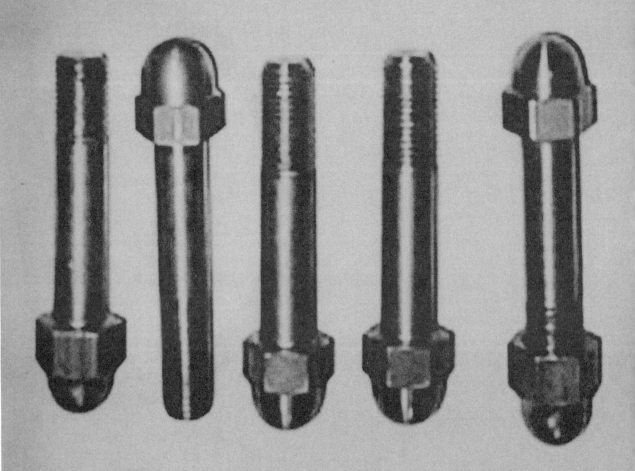

NYLON INSERT STOP

PANEL MOUNTING

CASTLE

REGULAR

HEX FLANGE NUTS

LOCK NUT

ASSEMBLING NUTS AND BOLTS

CH. 3

ASSEMBLING NUTS AND BOLTS

Face it. A mission project is far more complicated than loading up a van, driving to an amusement park, and setting your youth free. Even if you've been privileged to personally drive a bus full of sugar-buzzed roller coaster animals, a trip still isn't as simple as a one-day outing.

In fact, planning a mission project is more like a parent trying to assemble a bike on Christmas Eve. Everybody's watching. Everybody's waiting. And at some point it might be blindingly obvious that you don't have a clue what you're doing.

If you used the last chapter to think hard about your project—what you want to do and why—you've gone miles toward a smooth-running trip. This chapter offers practical help with the nitty-gritty. Whether you're tackling this project as a volunteer or as a paid church or parachurch staff member, here's more on what you need to get this monstrous job done.

YOUR TRIP TIMELINE AND TASKS

You might be able to pull off a summer mission project by booking your trip from your cell phone as you drive out of the church parking lot—but you'll be going who-knows-where to do who-cares-what. If your dreams for your trip are more specific than that, then you want to start planning early.

+ In the fall, many host groups open registrations, giving first choice to returning groups.

+ If you sign up before Christmas, you should still land more or less your pick of trips.

+ Right after the holidays slots fill rapidly.

+ By February many summer spots are gone.

+ During the spring you can still register for a trip. Spots often open up as churches take final headcounts and relinquish spots they had reserved. By this time, though, you aren't likely to get much latitude in what you do or where you go. You'll probably have to flex on your timing, and you might not be able to snare as many spots as you need, but it's not too late to try to book a growth-inducing trip. Shoot for a short starter trip—and remind yourself that taking your group late is better than never. Really.

You probably have a good idea of the all the pieces that go into planning a major youth group event, and the tasks are multitudinous indeed. For this whopper event, the major duties fall into four main groups. Here's what needs to happen—in lists that make for handy job descriptions:

INTEGRATION — OVERSEE AND NETWORK

+ Communicate with the host group

+ Communicate with the church

+ Field questions from parents and students

ADMINISTRATION — TRACK PAPERWORK AND FINANCES

+ Coordinate sign-ups, paperwork, finances, release forms, payment to the host group

+ Send notices and reminders—confirmation letters, meeting notices, room setups, and other arrangements

+ Oversee fundraising and scholarships (a job that might be big enough to stand on its own)

+ Reserve transportation and lodging, if needed

COMMUNICATION — GET THE WORD OUT BEFORE, DURING, AND AFTER THE PROJECT

 Publicize the trip using brochures, announcements, skits, and videos

 Organize prayer support via newsletters, a phone tree, or e-mail

TRAINING — EQUIP THE TEAM TO DO ITS BEST

 Determine preparation—covered in Chapter 4

 Gather information on where you're going

Prepare on-site teaching and worship as well as devotional material for kids—if not provided by your host group

Gather materials you'll need—tools, stuff to teach

Plan for follow-up with team members after your arrival home—the topic of Chapter 6

You can't do all this by yourself. In Chapter 2 you generated a list of possible helpers. Now is the time to start dividing up jobs—with everyone's consent, of course. You can draw on people like these for help:

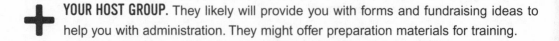 **YOUR TRIP'S LEADER.** As the person reading this book, here's your likely job. You probably need to be the point person who integrates your activity with the host group, church leadership, parents, and youth. You're the person who stands up front.

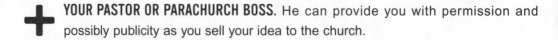 **YOUR HOST GROUP.** They likely will provide you with forms and fundraising ideas to help you with administration. They might offer preparation materials for training.

YOUR PASTOR OR PARACHURCH BOSS. He can provide you with permission and possibly publicity as you sell your idea to the church.

STUDENTS. Trip participants can easily pitch in with communication and administration. A few key students might want to be part of training.

+ SUPPORT STAFF. Your staff at church might be available to help with administration.

+ PARENTS AND OTHER ADULT VOLUNTEERS. These key helpers can take a load off you in administration, communication, and training. One or two might be willing to head up fundraising.

Delegating these jobs is necessary to get everything done—and it's part of building a support team of and for your youth.

In the last chapter you were pretty sure you had people to help you. Who are they? Jot their names here—and then go back to those tasks listed above and jot the name of a likely helper beside each.

_____

_____

_____

_____

_____

_____

GETTING THE WORD OUT

After you've secured your spots for a trip and started rounding up helpers, your first step is to create a brochure, but everything you want to say to your youth about the trip won't fit on one slip of paper. You'll need an informational meeting to tell about your upcoming project. Some hints:

+ GET THAT BROCHURE TOGETHER. People want the basics in their hands. Answer the questions budding journalists ask: Who? What? When? Where? Why? How much? You not only want to answer the question "What is it?" but "Why should I care?" If you've decided on any unusual requirements, radical rules, or mandatory group meetings before the trip—say, for training—note those on the brochure.

✚ **SCHEDULE A MEETING FOR BOTH YOUTH AND PARENTS—GIVING AT LEAST TWO WEEKS OF LEAD TIME.** Get at least two shots in the Sunday bulletin, preferably three, before you hold your meeting. Ditto for announcements in Sunday school and youth group. Call or accost youth you particularly want to join the trip.

✚ **MAKE THE MEETING CONVENIENT.** Sunday mornings immediately after church or following your midweek program are likely to guarantee your best attendance.

Then *make your meeting interesting.* Start your planning with material provided by the host group—brochures, a promo video, a speaker, whatever they can provide. Your goal is to provide both information and motivation, so do what you can to liven up the show, including skits or mime acting out what you do as well as commercials from teens who have already experienced mission trips.

Organize your thoughts on everything you want to say in an order that makes sense to you, but you may have the greatest impact if you start with a motivational piece—such as explaining why you want to do this project. Beware that at this first meeting you'll face a swirl of questions.

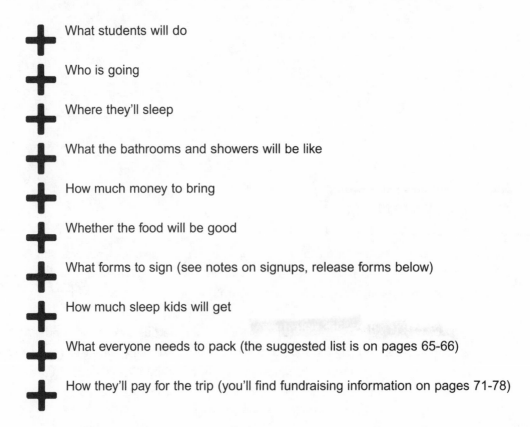

✚ What students will do

✚ Who is going

✚ Where they'll sleep

✚ What the bathrooms and showers will be like

✚ How much money to bring

✚ Whether the food will be good

✚ What forms to sign (see notes on signups, release forms below)

✚ How much sleep kids will get

✚ What everyone needs to pack (the suggested list is on pages 65-66)

✚ How they'll pay for the trip (you'll find fundraising information on pages 71-78)

+ What rules students will have to follow (don't miss **Rule of Thumb** on page 68)

+ How the team can be reached in an emergency

+ Safety and risks

+ How local folks will treat the group

The bottom line for youth is whether the trip will be any fun. Parents care about that too, but they want information on safety and the impact for their kids. Parents and youth both expect you to have answers. And you owe them answers. After all, you aren't crossing the street. You're taking these youth—maybe—to the other side of the planet. No matter where you're going you're probably taking them to a different world.

How are you going to figure out answers to every question? Again, if you've worked through the questions in the last chapter, you'll be astoundingly well prepared. But here are more sources for nuggets of knowledge to amaze your listeners:

+ **GET A REFERENCE.** Ask your host group for names of people you can talk to who have taken a trip with the host group.

+ **TALK TO A LOCAL.** Find someone from the place you're headed. Ask her what it's like there, especially for teens.

+ **TUNE INTO INTERNET RADIO BROADCASTS FROM YOUR DESTINATION.** With RealOne (www.real.com) or Windows Media Player (www.microsoft.com), you can tune in to local radio stations. Check www.comfm.com or www.live-radio.net for thorough listings.

+ **GO SEE FOR YOURSELF.** If you can swing the time and money, there's no substitute for scoping out your site firsthand. Bring back pictures and stories.

+ **DIG FOR INFORMATION.** If you're traveling to a foreign country, the U.S. Department of State provides Background Notes on every country in the world available at http://state.gov (a good site for homework too). Look around at http://travel.state.gov to find what you need to know about everything from shots to safe travel. Other sites to surf to:

+ Check the Travelers' Health section at www.cdc.gov.

+ The Web site www.frommers.com provides insight into destinations, health, and general travel guidance, all with a focus on budget travel.

+ Click on the Guides tab on www.expedia.com to find information on major urban destinations.

+ Destination Guides at www.travelocity.com include links to the ultrahip www.lonelyplanet.com. With the extensive and practical information presented, you'll be clued in on health data as well as rude things not to do in a particular culture.

One caution: In your enthusiasm to rally youth to the cause, don't make the whole of your presentation sound like a thumped-up Mountain Dew commercial. Present the riotous fun. But don't hide the sweaty hard work they'll do.

As you wrap up your meeting you'll want to have other vital information on hand—like how to sign up (more on that in a flash). You'll also want release forms and packing lists ready. You'll need those for distribution at the meeting or, if you're using an application process, to send to students once they've been accepted.

SIGN-UPS

By the time you finish your informational meeting you hopefully have motivated some youth to join you on your wacky adventure.

Whatever your system for signing up youth for other sorts of events, you'll undoubtedly need to nail down your participants sooner than you're used to. Host groups need a head count to save spots when you register. They'll want a deposit by an early date—a date that's the same for all groups or a date specific to your group, tied to the date you registered. Either way, your hosts will want a final count of youth and adults by late winter or early spring.

That means sign-ups can't drag it on forever. You want to get youth signed up and moving through the prep sessions discussed in the next chapter so your youth are prepared and pumped.

You'll want a sign-up form that asks for the usual name and address info. Unless you're absolutely positive your adult leaders will know every youth who signs up, have applicants include a picture.

Now you have to think about that big question you read about in the last chapter: Do you take everyone who wants to come or do students have to meet certain criteria?

Your sign-up sheet will need to spell out what you're looking for—the tougher the trip, the tougher the qualifications needed. Yet even if you're planning on taking everyone who applies, it's helpful to include some basic questions on the application—either to screen students who aren't ready for the trip or simply for your education. Your goal is to prod youth to ponder and answer questions like these:

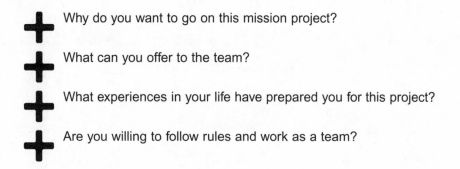

Why do you want to go on this mission project?

What can you offer to the team?

What experiences in your life have prepared you for this project?

Are you willing to follow rules and work as a team?

An application process with a few basic questions and a reasonable deadline sets a purposeful tone and gets commitments on paper, not letting students slide for months.

THE RELEASE FORM

Your church should already have a form it requires for events and trips—a form that includes emergency contact information for parents, a release of liability, and permission to seek medical attention. Your host group will also provide you with a detailed form of its own.

Because of the risks involved in many mission projects and the fact that you might find yourself in dire circumstances far from home, make sure your form includes a request for information on any medical condition that may impact participation or potentially endanger the student on the trip. That might sound overcautious—until a student shows up on a trip who swells up and could die if he gets poked in the stomach—and neither the student or parents tell you. It's happened.

MEDICAL RELEASE FORM

PLEASE PRINT IN INK:

Name:_____Age_____Birthday_____

Year in school_____ ☐ Male ☐ Female E-mail_____

Address_____ City_____State_____Zip_____

Phone_____Pager/Cell_____

Medical insurance company_____Policy #_____

Mother's name_____ Phone: Home_____ Work_____

Father's name_____ Phone: Home_____ Work_____

Emergency contact_____ Phone: Home_____ Work_____

MEDICAL HISTORY.

If necessary, describe in detail the nature and severity of any physical and / or psychological ailment, illness, propensity, weakness, limitation, handicap, disability, or condition to which your child is subject and of which the staff should be aware, and what, if any, action of protection is required on account thereof. Submit this notification in writing and attach it to this form. Include names of medications and dosages that must be taken.

_____has my permission to attend all

youth activities sponsored by (ORGANIZATION)_____

(hereinafter the "Church") from (DATE) _____ to (DATE)_____. This consent form

gives permission to seek whatever medical attention is deemed necessary, and releases the Church and its staff of any

liability against personal losses of named child.

Parent / guardian signature:_____Date:_____

PACKING LIST

Start with this tidy observation in mind: Most people pack too much.

Besides dealing with the mess of bringing more stuff than you need, your big consideration is space if you're driving and both space and weight if you're flying. You can go hardcore and pack what your adult leaders—female and male—consider reasonable and weigh it. But an easier way is to create a good packing list and tell everyone to stick to it. Students take their cue from the adults. If leaders are willing to rough it, then youth will realize they don't need to pack the house.

Pack in simple luggage that can be squashed and tossed—say, a duffle bag. Sleeping bags and pillows go in a stuff sack or hefty garbage bag—not loose and ready to unfurl.

Your host group will likely provide you with a packing list, but here's an authoritative sample from Adventures In Missions. This packing list is for a two-week trip overseas or to the interior of Mexico involving both work and relational evangelism. It comes with instructions to "modify the number of outfits as needed."

✚ 3 to 5 changes of work clothes—knee-length shorts or long pants and T-shirts. No gaping holes or stretched-out arm or leg holes. Halter tops, any type of sleeveless shirt, or cut off sleeves are not allowed.

✚ 3 to 5 changes of ministry clothes—skirts or dresses with slips for girls; long pants (no jeans) and a collar shirt for guys.

✚ Knee-length shorts for free time

✚ Underwear and socks

✚ 1 pair of sturdy work shoes (boots are highly recommended), 1 pair of sneakers or flats for skirts, 1 pair of shower shoes. No open-toed shoes for work or ministry.

✚ Modest swim suit

✚ PJs

✚ Washcloth and towel

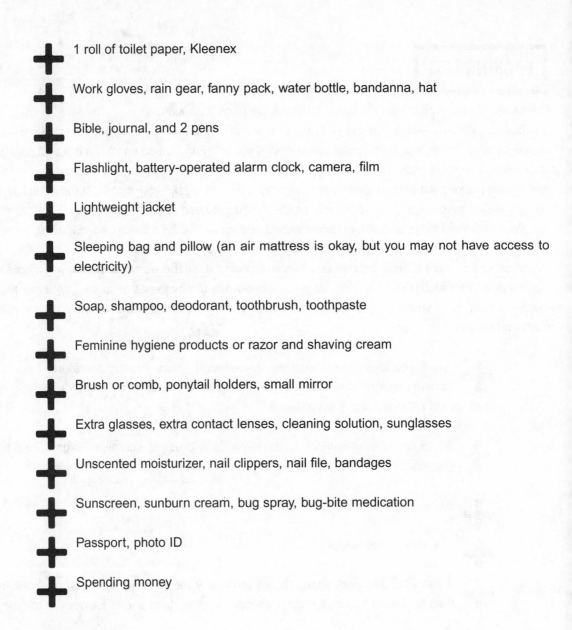

+ 1 roll of toilet paper, Kleenex

+ Work gloves, rain gear, fanny pack, water bottle, bandanna, hat

+ Bible, journal, and 2 pens

+ Flashlight, battery-operated alarm clock, camera, film

+ Lightweight jacket

+ Sleeping bag and pillow (an air mattress is okay, but you may not have access to electricity)

+ Soap, shampoo, deodorant, toothbrush, toothpaste

+ Feminine hygiene products or razor and shaving cream

+ Brush or comb, ponytail holders, small mirror

+ Extra glasses, extra contact lenses, cleaning solution, sunglasses

+ Unscented moisturizer, nail clippers, nail file, bandages

+ Sunscreen, sunburn cream, bug spray, bug-bite medication

+ Passport, photo ID

+ Spending money

ADULT PACKING

While you're thinking about packing: The adult leaders on your trip will want a backpack that's hand-carried as you travel—and maybe kept with you wherever you go, depending on the advice of your host. Treat this backpack with the importance of the briefcase carried by Secret Service for the U.S. president, the one with launch codes for nuclear weapons. Inside you'll want to stash the most important items:

+ *Passports* if required for your destination.

+ *Release/medical forms* for each participant, including emergency contact info.

+ *Emergency phone numbers* compiled to one list—your host group's main offices, phone numbers of parents, and life-or-death phone numbers from your host specific to your location. If you are traveling out of your home country, know how to reach your embassy.

+ *Emergency cash.* Unless your hosts advise otherwise, have students carry their own cash.

+ *Medications.* Depending on your destination and the maturity of your students, you might choose to have leaders carry the prescription drugs your students need—from asthma medicine to bee-sting kits to Ritalin.

If you're going for more than a weekend and you'll be more than 10 minutes from a 24-hour convenience store, you can pack an assortment of over-the-counter medications such as pain relievers; nausea, diarrhea, and motion-sickness medications; decongestant; cough drops; tissues; sunburn spray; hygiene products; antibiotic ointment; and bandages. Even better, pack a nurse. If you have a group big enough to need more than three adults, it's great to have someone with medical training.

And grown-ups, give yourselves a break. If you have the space, bring your favorite pillow and an air mattress—an inflatable bed or Thermarest sleeping pad takes up minimal room and makes for much happier leaders.

TRAVEL AND MEDICAL INFORMATION

If you need passports for your destination, your host group will likely coach you through the process of getting passports and other travel documents. But if you want to get a head start—or you want to sound sophisticated—you can access information on the Web. American citizens can check http://travel.state.gov/passport_services.html. Canada's official passport Web page is www.dfaitmaeci.gc.ca/passport. Your host group or a travel agent can provide you with details on obtaining a visa—your entry permit, not a credit card—for foreign destinations.

And if you want to doublecheck what shots are recommended for travel to other countries, the Centers for Disease Control offers "what to know before you go" at www.cdc.gov/travel.

RULE OF THUMB

THE MINIMUM STANDARD YOU SET FOR YOUTH ON ANY TRIP ARE OBVIOUS: BEHAVE AND DON'T BASH EACH OTHER. YOUR YOUTH REPRESENT THEMSELVES, THE GROUP, YOUR CHURCH, AND GOD. YOU WANT TO CREATE AN UPLIFTING ENVIRONMENT.

BUT ON A SHORT-TERM PROJECT, YOU NEED EVEN MORE. THE TRIP IS MORE CHALLENGING, AND YOU MIGHT BE HEADED INTO A SEMI-DANGEROUS SETTING. IF YOU ANTICIPATE STUDENTS MAY HAVE A TOUGH TIME FOLLOWING THE RULES, SPELL THEM OUT CLEARLY FROM THE BEGINNING—IN YOUR INFORMATIONAL MEETING OR EVEN ON YOUR BROCHURE AND SIGN-UP SHEET. DON'T MAKE THE TRIP A DOWNER, BUT SELL THE STUDENTS IN ADVANCE ON THE COOPERATION YOU'LL NEED TO MAKE THE TRIP WORK. YOUR HOST GROUP MIGHT PROVIDE A HEFTY SET OF RULES FOR YOUTH TO FOLLOW.

HERE ARE SOME ISSUES YOU'LL WANT TO ANTICIPATE:

+ CAN YOUTH COME LATE TO THE PROJECT, LEAVE THE TRIP AND COME BACK, OR GO HOME EARLY?

+ IS ATTENDING PREPARATION AND FOLLOW-UP SESSIONS MANDATORY?

+ HOW ARE YOU GOING TO PAY FOR THIS TRIP? MORE ON FUNDRAISING LATER ON THIS CHAPTER—BUT WHAT IF A STUDENT HATES FUNDRAISING AND HIS PARENTS JUST WANT TO WRITE A CHECK?

+ HOW ARE YOU GOING TO HANDLE GUY-GIRL PAIRING OFF?

+ WHAT KIND OF READING MATERIAL CAN YOUTH BRING?

+ HOW ABOUT MEDIA AND MUSIC? ARE PORTABLE ELECTRONICS ALLOWED ON THE TRIP AT ALL? HOW ABOUT WHEN YOU'RE TRAVELING?

+ WHAT CLOTHES ARE APPROPRIATE? MANY HOST GROUPS BAN SPAGHETTI STRAPS OR TANK TOPS. (IT'S EASIEST TO JUST SAY, "BRING T-SHIRTS.") MOST WILL ALSO SPECIFY ONE-PIECE SWIMSUITS FOR THE GIRLS. IN MANY SETTINGS YOU'LL ALSO WANT STUDENTS TO DITCH DESIGNER LABELS AND TEAM LOGOS. KEEP IN MIND THAT PRICEY OR EVEN SPOTLESSLY NEW CLOTHING MAY SET YOU APART FROM THE PEOPLE YOU MINISTER TO.

+ DO YOUTH KEEP TRACK OF PRESCRIPTION AND OVER-THE-COUNTER MEDICATIONS OR DO YOU WANT TO DISPENSE THEM?

+ HOW MUCH PRIMPING IS ALLOWED? ONE EASY RULE IS TO BAN BLOW DRYERS AND CURLING IRONS.

+ ENCOURAGE MINIMAL MAKEUP.

+ HOW WILL SLEEPING HOURS BE ENFORCED?

+ ARE BEEPERS OR CELL PHONES ALLOWED?

+ HOW MUCH SPENDING MONEY DO YOUTH NEED? FIGURE OUT A RECOMMENDED MAXIMUM—ENOUGH FOR MEALS ON THE TRIP AS WELL AS SNACKS AND SOUVENIRS IF THEY'RE AVAILABLE ONSITE. BRINGING MORE INCREASES THE RISK OF THEFT OR LOSS.

+ CAN STUDENTS PACK SNACKS? EXPECT SOME EXTENSIVE STASHES OF JUNK FOOD UNLESS YOU SAY OTHERWISE.

+ IF YOU'RE TRAVELING TO A FOREIGN LOCATION, YOU'LL NEED TO GIVE ADDITIONAL GUIDELINES ABOUT DRINKING THE WATER AND BUYING FOOD ON THE STREET. THE CENTERS FOR DISEASE CONTROL OFFER A SIMPLE RULE WHEN TRAVELING IN FOREIGN COUNTRIES: "BOIL IT, COOK IT, PEEL IT, OR FORGET IT." IN OTHER WORDS, EAT ONLY THOROUGHLY COOKED FOOD YOU HAVE PEELED YOURSELF. SEE STAYING HEALTHY (PAGE 70) FOR MORE GUIDELINES TO AVOID GETTING SICK.

WHAT ADDITIONAL RULES FOR STUDENTS DO I FEEL COMPELLED TO INCLUDE?

_____

_____

_____

_____

STAYING HEALTHY

ON MANY MISSION PROJECTS YOUR BIGGEST PROBLEM IS STUDENTS WHO GET SICK, AND YOUR BIGGEST WORRY IS COOKING YOUR KIDS—BAKING THEM IN THE SUN AND NOT GETTING THEM ENOUGH WATER.

BELIEVE IT OR DON'T, YOU CAN GET A GROUP OF YOUTH THROUGH A WHOLE SUMMER OVERSEAS WITHOUT ANY MAJOR ILLNESS. YOU MIGHT CHOOSE TO MODIFY THESE GUIDELINES, BUT THEY'RE SOLID ADVICE NO MATTER THE DESTINATION:

- KEEP A WATER BOTTLE HANDY IN HOT CLIMATES.

- WASH HANDS OFTEN WITH SOAP AND WATER.

- GET ADEQUATE SLEEP.

IF YOU'RE TRAVELING TO UNDERDEVELOPED AREAS, ADD THESE:

- DRINK ONLY BOTTLED OR BOILED WATER OR CARBONATED DRINKS IN CANS OR BOTTLES. AVOID TAP WATER, FOUNTAIN DRINKS, AND ICE CUBES.

- KNOW HOW TO ASK FOR BEVERAGES WITHOUT ICE.

- BOIL IT, COOK IT, PEEL IT, OR FORGET IT.

- WATCH OUT FOR UNDERCOOKED GROUND BEEF AND POULTRY, RAW EGGS, AND UNPASTEURIZED DAIRY PRODUCTS.

- DON'T EAT FOOD PURCHASED FROM STREET VENDORS. DON'T EAT FOOD JUST BECAUSE A MISSIONARY WHO'S BEEN IN THE FIELD FOR 40 YEARS CAN STOMACH IT.

- KEEP FEET CLEAN AND DRY, AND DON'T GO BAREFOOT UNLESS YOU REALLY WANT INTESTINAL WORMS.

- DON'T FEED OR PET THE ANIMALS—ESPECIALLY MONKEYS, DOGS, AND CATS—TO AVOID LICE, BITES, AND LITTLE DISEASES LIKE RABIES AND THE PLAGUE. IN MANY PARTS OF THE WORLD, THE POOCH STARING YOU DOWN ISN'T A FAMILY PET.

PAYING FOR YOUR TRIP

One final detail you'll need to talk about at your informational meeting: How are you going to get the money for your project?

To be honest, the biggest, hardest part of getting from here to there is often fundraising.

Big question: So how are you going to do it?

Bigger question: Do you have to?

If this is your church's first mission project, here's a huge hunk of wisdom: The trip needs to be about the trip. That means don't make your biggest worry fundraising. Make your first priority going—getting your students somewhere doing something good. While you want a project distant enough or adventurous enough to capture their imagination, your best option for a first trip is a low-hassle, low-cost trip that won't bust the budget.

One reason to save fundraising for second- or third-year groups is that once youth know firsthand they absolutely want to be involved with short-term mission projects, then you can get them to buy into the idea of fundraising and more extensive preparation—two ingredients for going further and doing more. After your group has an impacting experience, you can easily sell bigger ideas: "Let's go further," "Let's work harder," "Let's pull the money together to do something even bigger," "Let's train as a team so we're really ready."

Don't assume that doing a trip automatically means you have to jump into fundraising mode. Think first about these options:

✚ **DON'T SPEND IT.** The difference in costs from group to group and from project to project can be startling. People from parents to students to board members will demand to know why you want to spend $3,000 per student for a 10-day trip to Africa instead of $200 per head for a six-day project to the inner city. While cost shouldn't be the only factor in choosing a group, low-cost options do exist. You can choose another project. Because transportation is a major portion of many trips, you get more bang for your buck by extending your stay. And you can cut costs by going simple—by borrowing vans instead of using pricey rentals or taking a school bus instead of a motor coach.

✚ **SELF-FUNDED.** What could be tidier? Set a price and collect checks. There might be youth in your group who make more money per hour selling dogs or serving tables than some adults make at their grown-up jobs. Or you might have youth whose parents can easily write a check for whatever dollar amount their children need—and for several others as well. You might judge that your youth have adequate disposable income to pay for the trip strictly out-of-pocket.

While asking youth to self-fund a trip can be a barrier, some churches see it as a necessary part of the discipline and discipleship of being on the trip. If youth know about the trip by mid-winter, they can jump into babysitting, caddying, mowing lawns, selling newspapers, or working on a farm. Older youth can get cash through their normal part-time jobs.

Remember the downside: Not all students have access to high-paying jobs or disposable family income. Some will have a tough time scraping together a hundred dollars. When the price of your project rises to a few hundred dollars or a few thousand dollars, you'll surely have students who need help coming up with the cash. Even in the most affluent churches, you can assume some students find money difficult to come by.

✝ **CHURCH BUDGET.** Some church boards have entirely funded trips—modestly priced trips, of course. It can be tough to predict how your church will react to requests for funding—whether your pastor and board will encourage self-funding and self-reliance or be so ecstatic to see the youth finally doing something they will underwrite most of the trip. Beware that money available one year might be gone the next.

Churches providing partial funding often do so in three ways:

✝ Scholarships based on need.

✝ A flat dollar amount or percentage toward the trip for all students.

✝ Matching an amount paid by your participants.

Picking up the trip cost for all adult leaders is another approach to making a contribution for the trip. (If your church can't spring for that part of your costs, build the expense into the price you set for each student.)

At some fuzzy dollar amount, your trip will become too expensive to pinch any more pennies, self-fund, or even hope that your church board can produce the cash. Yet if your group is convinced they want to take a particular trip, the kids will be awesomely creative at raising funds.

ROLLING INTO FUNDRAISING

If you and your students are ready to tackle the task of fundraising, you'll want to back up and ask yourself what role fundraising plays in your trip. Despite all outward appearances, fundraising isn't just about money. It's part of the learning experience—and the return you want from all your hard work will be totally obvious to your youth. You want your students to grow in—

DEPENDENCE ON GOD. You no doubt want your students to realize that missions isn't about getting a freebie ride to a far off place but rather that God is the source of every gift.

PRAYERFULNESS. You can learn to tell God about your needs, to talk to him about your purposes for going, to thank him for every dollar that shows up.

DISCIPLINE AND SERVANTHOOD. You don't have to be a crab who says, "Back when I was your age, we had to work hard for our money" to know that the money-raising process can teach students about sacrifice and hard work. In an affluent congregation you might choose to limit the percentage of the trip that can be paid by parents. Require students to earn the money themselves, join group fundraising, or reach out to individual supporters.

MISSIONS AWARENESS. You might be in a church that knows little about missions of any kind. Your trip might bring a sudden burst of awareness. Think hard about publicizing your trip widely and doing some community-building fundraising even if you can get the money from other sources.

POSITIVE PUBLICITY FOR YOUR YOUTH. Face it. Youth doing good in the world can radically remake some congregation member's view of youth and youth ministry.

CASH. Getting hold of the money is, of course, still part of the purpose of fundraising. How big of a part is it for you?

If we've decided that fundraising is a necessary part of your trip, what are our goals for the money-raising process? Of all the side benefits of fundraising, which are most important to us?

_____

_____

_____

_____

_____

_____

AVOIDING A SUCKING SOUND

If all you're interested in is getting cash, people will soon hear a sucking sound as you walk by mooching their money. Whether or not your fundraising efforts are a wretched turn-off to everyone who knows you and your youth has to do with attitude.

+ **PLAN A GREAT PROJECT.** No trick will raise money for a trip too stupid for people to willingly invest in. Kyle's grandparents might write a check for anything Kyle wants to do for God, but more rational folks in your congregation won't. Be a good steward with solid plans for your project, however, and the money will show up.

+ **GIVE SOMETHING IN RETURN.** Start by thinking about the people who might provide funds. What encouragement can you provide them? How can you keep them informed so they feel like an integral part of the trip? What benefits will accrue to the church as a whole? A trip is a big investment. People want their investments to pay off.

+ **SAY THANKS.** Fundraising doesn't stop when coins clank in a can. At the very least plot a team-wide plan for sending thank-yous. More appropriate is a detailed report or a meeting for supporters to give a full account of the completed project.

Once you've committed to fundraising, explore the three main strategies:

✚ APPEALS TO THE CONGREGATION. Your church can present everything from special offerings to an entire service geared around the mission. Host an informational meeting about the trip for the congregation. Put articulate youth in front of the congregation giving updates about the preparations. Slip information about the project into church newsletters. Once you've done a trip, you can make special appeals to alumni and parents.

✚ INDIVIDUAL SUPPORT RAISING. The thought of sending out letters requesting monetary support might make your youth squirm. But inviting people to participate in a trip doesn't have to sound like begging, and the request doesn't need to promise bodily healing to givers or threaten the wrath of God on those who choose not to give.

Start by checking with your church about policy related to appeals for support. Too many requests for money compete with regular giving and support of career missionaries; your church may limit you to sending letters outside the congregation.

You can send a whole-team letter from you to people on the church mailing list, but you can help youth stretch their comfort zones by mailing their wider network of family and friends outside the church.

You can provide sample letters (in electronic format so kids don't have to start from scratch and letters can be easily personalized). As you compose your letter, keep in mind these ingredients of a great support-raising letter:

✚ INFORMATION. Explain where and when you're going and what you hope to accomplish. Tell how you'll prepare—and what you can offer.

✚ INSPIRATION. Your plans are no doubt inspiring, but you can also provide a daily reminder—a bookmark, team photo, or a Web address with up-to-date news on your project.

✚ INVITATION. Hinting that you need money isn't as effective as honestly asking. Invite them to be a part of your ministry, and give instructions for sending tax-deductible gifts.

✚ GROUP FUNDRAISING. Your third option is to dive into fundraising events as a team. Count on lots of work. But if you do it right, you'll reap loads of fun—and enough cash to get you where you're going.

You can spend a lot of effort and see little return on your effort, so find a parent or other church member with some business savvy to help you sort through fundraising opportunities. You'll want to revisit your goals for raising money, evaluating possibilities for teambuilding among students, involvement of your church, missions awareness, and crowd appeal. You're also aiming for good taste. You're not buying uniforms for the high school cheerleading squad, so skip the bikini car washes. The success of any given fundraiser varies from place to place, church to church, and even year to year. Pay attention to what has worked in your area before, but here are some basics:

+ *Pancake breakfast, box lunch, or spaghetti dinner.* The hope is that people will not only attend but also give above and beyond the cost.

+ *School ideas.* You can swipe ideas from schools fundraisers: candy, half-baked or build-your-own pizzas, cheese and sausage, cookie dough.

+ *_____-a-thons.* Fill in the blank. You can run, walk, swim, pray, read the Bible, collect trash, live in a cardboard box—all with flat donations or based on the duration of your activity. You get extra credit for doing something worthwhile at the same time.

+ *Bake sale.* Items can include breads, cookies, cakes, pies, and more. You can have students do the baking or bring dad's. Try a pie-in-the-youth-pastor's-face for audience involvement.

+ *Rummage sale.* You can ring up more profits if you also offer baked goods, candy, or more substantial eats.

+ *Rent-a-youth.* Hire out your students for specific tasks or for anything not immoral or illegal.

+ *White elephant auction.* Auction off your most useless stuff—a congregation-wide junk swap that can be repeated annually.

+ *Corporate appeals.* Ask people inside and outside your church to provide items for a silent auction. Donations can come from manufacturers, restaurants, retailers, or service providers.

+ *Car wash.* You might do better if you sell coupons ahead of time.

+ *Web site.* While you might not go so far as to take donations via credit or debit cards, you can post information that generates interest and potential funds for your trip. Keep it fresh with news and prayer requests while you're away.

+ *Change collection.* Do something useful with all those pennies that accumulate—though make it clear you won't refuse nickels, dimes, quarters, or dollar bills.

+ *Golf tournament.* In some settings a fundraising golf tournament works. Ask around with your golfers!

+ *Creative activities.* Run your idea by the local fun police before proceeding: cow chip tosses, cow pie bingo, donkey basketball.

WHEN YOU'VE TAPPED OUT CAR WASHES AND CANDY BARS AND NEED MORE IDEAS FOR FUNDRAISING, CHECK OUT THESE RESOURCES:

+ *GREAT FUNDRAISING IDEAS FOR YOUTH GROUPS* (YOUTH SPECIALTIES, 1993) OFFERS OVER 150 EASY-TO-USE MONEYMAKERS THAT WORK.

+ *ADMINISTRATION, PUBLICITY, & FUNDRAISING* (YOUTH SPECIALTIES, 1997) PROVIDES MORE THAN 250 TIME-SAVING TIPS AND CREATIVE IDEAS TO ORGANIZE, PROMOTE, AND FUND YOUR MINISTRY, WITH MANY IDEAS THAT APPLY TO YOUR MISSION PROJECT.

BOTH BOOKS GIVE YOU PROVEN IDEAS TO HELP YOU RAISE THE CASH YOU NEED.

Finally, you need to decide how you will distribute the money you make. You can require each student to work equal hours and distribute the money equally, or you can let students choose how much or how little they want to participate—and earn—since you total the number of hours contributed by all youth, divide the total amount earned by the total number of hours to find the hourly rate, and distribute by the number of hours each worked.

Your choice probably depends on a larger goal—whether you want to build a sense of team or a sense of personal responsibility.

What are my initial thoughts on fundraising? How should I go about getting the money that will get us from here to there?

_____

_____

_____

_____

_____

How will I distribute the money we make?

_____

_____

_____

_____

_____

PULLING IT ALL TOGETHER

When you've tightened down the last of these nuts and bolts, you're undoubtedly relieved. But there's one more thing you need to do before your trip. It's crucial. Read on.

CH.4

ADY TO GO

CH. **4**

GETTING READY TO GO

Suppose, for a minute, that you're two months out from plunging into your short-term trip. Maybe you're already there. Or maybe you're past that point. But you're so busy pulling together the nuts-and-bolts details of the trip that you'll scream if someone asks you to do one more thing.

Pssst. Your students want one more thing.

Your youth aren't particularly concerned about nitty-gritty trip details. They're not excited about checking off proper forms and filing them in alphabetical order. For most of them their first thought isn't even the big-picture goal of spreading God's Good News about Jesus throughout the world. To the extent that they're thinking about the trip—and at the moment they might not be—they're wondering how the trip will go, whether they'll like the whole experience, what exactly they'll be doing.

Think about it: Your group might be headed somewhere way beyond your students' ability to wrap their brain around—to the inner city, a reservation, an impoverished mountain community, a border town, or deep into a foreign country. Your students will be doing something they've maybe never tried. And they'll be serving together in a unique group that's maybe never before assembled.

So how can a group thrive during such a one-of-a-kind experience?

Preparation.

Just as a football team practices day after day before they ever square off in a real game, your group needs to get ready.

Setting out on a short-term trip with a group that's unprepared is like fielding a football team that's never practiced before. It can be done, because your players have a general idea of what the game is about. But there's a good chance you'll get slaughtered on the scoreboard—except that on a mission trip the stakes are infinitely higher than winning or losing a ball game. Preparation is the only way you'll work together to seamlessly run plays. And whether or not your students ask for it out loud, they're looking for real-world, real-life training.

WHY BOTHER TO GET READY?

You're not hitting the field to take on 300-pound, body-crushing linebackers. So what exactly do you have to gain by preparing? Why bother with anything but moving students straight to a project—and as quickly as possible?

+ PREPARATION RAISES REAL ISSUES. Lots of the problems you'll face on a short-term mission trip are predictable, and preparation helps you skirt loads of difficulties. When tough times come your way, you've at least built yourself an entry point for talking openly with your team—as in, "Remember when I said this would be an adventure? Well…"

+ PREPARATION SETS EXPECTATIONS. Students need to know the ground rules for your time together—what's okay, what's not, what you're trying to accomplish. Good prep work sets the tone for your whole trip. If you don't help students develop realistic expectations for the trip, they'll develop their own—perhaps unrealistic—expectations, which is a setup for disappointment.

+ PREPARATION SETS STUDENTS AT EASE. For youth who are wired to analyze and dissect a situation before they dive in, you'll put them at ease if you give them ample information and a preview of the experience. And for youth who like to dive in and do, you'll be giving them the up-front guidance they'll need whether they acknowledge it or not.

+ PREPARATION FOCUSES THE TEAM ON THE TASK. To continue the football analogy, preparation ensures everyone is working off the same page of the playbook. Students, parents, hosts, nationals, and leaders all bring a load of dreams and desires. Preparation helps everyone work toward the same goal.

+ PREPARATION EQUIPS. You might be working at a project where you don't need to bring a bag of special skills. Then again, you might be doing something that requires thorough training or rehearsal. Even if your task doesn't take special expertise, your group still needs to practice working together as a team.

+ PREPARATION BUILDS ENDURANCE. Youth feel like they've had the wind knocked out of them when they're jarred by a hit they never saw coming, but your youth can endure if they're prepared. Short-term trips can not only put your students in challenging external circumstances, but they also put your students face-to-face with internal ugliness, including selfishness, laziness, and apathy.

Chapters 7 through 10 of this book contain four sessions to help you train your students to do their best, but before you grab your calendar and ink time for prep sessions, it pays to think a bit more about what your group will need.

HOW MUCH PREPARATION DO WE NEED?

You can pursue two extremes of preparation:

+ UNDERDONE. Some host groups won't require your team to do any preparation—mental, physical, relational, or spiritual—before you show up. You hop in the church van and unload on site. The approach definitely won't maximize what you accomplish.

+ OVERDONE. You can engage in months of longwinded meetings, making a church's year-round youth ministry revolve around a mission trip—not around a focus on evangelism or missions or service, but the process of planning and executing a single trip. While that sounds like a grand idea, it pushes aside other important growth opportunities for youth. It also loses their attention and kills the enthusiasm of students who want to get out and do something for God.

So where's the balance? How much preparation do you need? The longer or more intense the trip, the greater your need for preparation. Some rule-of-thumb minimums:

+ Set aside an hour or two of preparation for a weekend project.

+ Commit to a day or two for a week-long trip.

+ You could easily spend a full week or two grooming a team for a summerlong project.

Preparing your students for the most effective project possible doesn't have to overwhelm you or them. The four prep sessions in this kit are ideal to get your group ready for a typical one-week project. You can also pick and choose among these sessions for shorter trips, and you can stretch the activities to lengthen and strengthen your training considerably. You can work though this material with your students in a variety of ways:

+ FOUR SESSIONS. One format is to schedule four hour-and-a-half sessions—mandatory for all participants—spread over the weeks before your trip.

+ WEEKEND RETREAT. You could instead cover all four lessons on a retreat a few weeks prior to your trip.

+ START OF YOUR TRIP. The easiest route—and the only one actually guaranteed to get all your participants present—is to use the lessons as the basis of a one- or two-day training session immediately before you leave for your trip.

Adding a retreat or a couple days for preparation to your trip doesn't have to be expensive. If you house participants at your church, for example, or at a rustic, inexpensive setting like a state park campsite, adding training time gets you more days together and more impact on your group at minimal cost.

GIVING YOUR STUDENTS THE RIGHT PREPARATION

Prepping for a mission trip is like packing a backpack for a weeklong hike. Put in the right stuff, and you'll be a happy camper. Head for the woods minus the goodies and you'll spend a week fighting mosquitoes and massaging blisters.

Take it from travel guru Arthur Frommer, who made this pointed remark about the necessity of trip preparation—and he wasn't even thinking about the utter importance of a trip aimed at missions: "I continue to be dismayed by the sight of people embarking for a trip with reservations, vouchers, policies of insurance, rail tickets, advance theatre seats, converters and adapters—but without a notion as to the political outlook, culture, history or theology of the people they are about to visit."

It's foolish to take care of all the practical details of a trip yet fail to do what you can ahead of time to maximize the growth of youth, the good of others, and the glory of God.

All participants in short-term missions need a few basics to get ready to go. None is huge news, but without packing into your students any one of these necessities, your trip will be far less than it could be.

As you look through the four areas of necessary preparation, think about what your group already knows—better yet, evaluate what your group already lives. Ponder the stuff they've gotten not only into their heads but also their hearts and actions.

Prep sessions aren't the only place students gain this missions know-how. It's handed down by tradition—through the expectations of older youth who've participated in previous projects. Some of it might be cultivated by week-in, week-out service at home, and some of it happens through group building you do at regular weekly meetings or on retreats. Formal preparation ensures that students come to a trip as ready as they can be. They'll need information and experience in four key areas:

1. YOUTH NEED A PICTURE OF WHERE THEY'RE HEADED.

When Jesus came to earth, he was no gawking tourist. God had scouted the planet. He knew his creation totally. He comprehended our problems completely. He understood the particulars of the human condition in infinite detail.

Unlike Jesus, your students won't know everything about the place where you're headed until they actually go—and even then it would take them years to truly understand a place. But they don't have to go clueless. While nothing will replace the experience of getting to a mission site and seeing it with their own eyes, the first thing your youth need from you is a picture of where they're headed.

Prep Session 1 (page 128) offers ideas to help you and your students find out about where you're going. The session rallies the team for an adventure, sets forth expectations. It shows you how to give an overview of the trip—and a last chance to turn back.

2. YOUTH NEED A GRASP OF THEIR MISSION.

Your students may or may not be well-versed in the fact that Jesus commanded us to go into the world in his name. They might not have connected their going with their own growth, others' good, and God's glory. But without a basic understanding of the big whys of going on short-term missions, participants aren't ready to roll.

As you go for God, you want your students to know what makes this trip different from a vacation. They need to understand what makes this Christian project different from volunteer opportunities they might have experienced through Scouts, community groups, or public schools—even if the groups do much of the same stuff. **Prep Session 2** (page 140) helps you explain what you'll be doing, why you're going, and what God has to do with it.

After **Prep Session 2** you might also choose to incorporate sessions of your own to prepare participants for tasks that require planning or special skill. (If you're teaching a vacation Bible school, for example, you'll need to plan lessons, music, crafts, et cetera. If you're doing construction, you might want to get a skilled worker in to teach you the tricks of the trade. Or if you're doing an evangelistic outing on bikes, you'll want to get your backsides on a bike and work with the students on talking to non-Christians.)

The end of Prep Session 2 includes resources for picking up the skills you need.

3. YOUTH NEED TO COMMIT TO SERVING.

On a short-term mission project, there's no way to predict what opportunities might pop up—or what difficulties might threaten to demolish your group. The quality of your trip through the highs and lows of a mission project will be vastly improved if youth think about potential hard times in advance—and make a choice to commit to your goals for the trip.

Prep Session 3 (page 154) teaches students to make the trip a chance to act as servants. Spending some time addressing this topic is the key that gives youth the ability to do whatever it takes to get the job done. Real commitment takes time to buy into. So while you may or may not want to have your students sign a formal covenant or agreement to give their all on the trip, the goal of Prep Session 3 is to entice students to rise to whatever your trip demands.

4. YOUTH NEED PRACTICE WORKING TOGETHER.

There's no quicker way to undo a mission trip than not getting along as a group. If you manage to get loads of work done despite yourselves, your great work is ruined for anyone watching by the bad attitudes of students and leaders.

You've probably got one set of students feeling timid about the trip and another wanting to run the show. You've likely got guys and girls, students old and young, maybe a few siblings who never get along at home. Almost for sure you've got a group that has never worked together. For each person on the team—what might be a wild mix of participants—you need to answer the question, "How are we all going to get along?"

Prep Session 4 (page 168) helps you build the teamwork now that you'll need later.

USING THE PREP SESSIONS

The sessions in this kit don't script every word you should say during a meeting. They require your thoughtful input and planning. So take the time to make the lessons your own, a custom fit for your group and its project. That said, here are some other tips for making the most of the prep sessions:

✚ **PLAN.** The best start to your group's preparation is your own careful preparation of sessions. Read through the lessons. Weigh options. Mull the needs of individual students and the group as a whole. Then pick activities that fit the time you have allotted.

✚ **MOVE.** Don't trap your students in a Sunday school room. Your trip will show them how God is actively working in the world. That requires leaving home and familiar surroundings. So start now! Mix it up. Find getaway spots—a park pavilion, someone's house, even the basement of an inner city church. Moving around encourages adaptability. You can get more done with your group by taking them on a 45-minute hike and having a quick follow-up chat than you might accomplish through week after week of discussions. As an added bonus, you'll find out now who can follow directions and show up on time.

+ STRETCH—OR SHRINK. Any one of these sessions could be the basis of a retreat—or fit into a little more than an hour. Use what your group needs and lose the rest.

+ ADAPT. This kit contains everything from time-tested activities like a trust walk to ideas you might not have tried before. Beginner-level or advanced, simple or complicated—take your pick. You know your youth. Don't do stuff they would gag on, but remember that you may need to stretch your own expectations and attitudes as much as your students do. If you've done a lot of training and teambuilding with your group before, don't abandon your proven preparation activities.

Each session breaks into several components. Some reasons for each:

+ GET IT GOING. The Sacred Cone of Learning says people remember significantly more if they do something, so sessions begins with an opener—an activity that primes your group to learn. If you have the time, combining these activities can form the basis for all-day or overnight retreats.

+ TALK IT THROUGH. Processing transforms an activity into a learning event. Each session offers ideas for guided discussion. The goal is to get students thinking and talking not only about the activity but also about how it applies to life and their upcoming trip. If they're reluctant to talk, let them know you need their input—then realize they're usually learning even if they're tight-lipped.

+ GET IT FROM THE WORD. What does the Bible say about the topic du jour? Your group may whip out their Bibles and notebooks as easily as they dig for quarters to plug into the church Coke machine. For other groups, Bible study is a stretch. Don't neglect the Bible. It's both inspiration and instruction for all you'll do. Each lesson provides a key passage and several cross-references. To encourage interaction and teamwork, the format of these Bible studies is discussion-based—questions and answers—rather than stand up and talk at them. You can cultivate participation by drawing out answers, then drawing conclusions.

+ PRAY IT UP. Each session includes a prayer focus that lists several Bible passages for what is sometimes called Scripture praying. These verses can inspire prayer in a variety of forms, from simple, one-line prayers that ask, "God, do this stuff in us" to intense prayers for the ministry of your trip.

+ WRAP IT UP. Here's the spot to give your group those last-minute announcements you don't want them to forget.

+ TAKE IT HOME. God's preparation of your group doesn't have to stop with the few hours you spend during these sessions. This section lists optional ways your group can apply lessons in everyday life.

STILL SCRATCHIN' YOUR NOGGIN?

You might have all the details of your trip nailed down and still be pondering whether your group truly needs preparation. But no team can get around it. Even if your group has participated in numerous trips, preparation pulls you all together to function your best for this project. If you're still wondering, think of preparation like this: It's a way to say, "We need to get focused on the task at hand," and "We still don't have all the answers."

What will challenge us most where we're headed?

_____

_____

_____

_____

Need some ideas? Here are some external and internal battles your team might face. Circle the ones you think might be challenges.

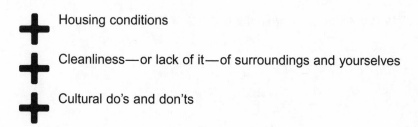

+ Housing conditions

+ Cleanliness—or lack of it—of surroundings and yourselves

+ Cultural do's and don'ts

✚ Tasks that don't seem fair or fun

✚ Getting along

✚ Lack of personal space and privacy

✚ Spiritual opposition

✚ Disinterest

✚ Heat or cold

✚ Rain or drought

✚ Working together

Given these probable battles, what kind of preparation do we need most? Circle the two areas below that name your biggest needs. That doesn't mean you ignore other areas, but that you make the most of those particular prep sessions.

✚ Orientation to where we're going (Prep Session 1)

✚ Keeping focused on our mission (Prep Session 2)

✚ Giving with a servant attitude (Prep Session 3)

✚ Working together as a team (Prep Session 4)

Are there any practical, task-oriented skills we need to practice to do our job right?

_____

_____

_____

_____

How many sessions do we need to master those skills? What would we cover during each session?

_____

_____

_____

_____

_____

Will we require adult trip leaders to participate in all training sessions?

_____

_____

_____

_____

_____

PULLING IT TOGETHER

With all the tasks you need to accomplish to get your group wherever you're headed, it's tempting to say, "Just show up on the morning of the trip. We'll hop on the bus and think about what we're doing when we get there." Your students won't have a picture of where they're headed. They'll show up with mixed motivations. They might not put on the towel and reach out with Christ-like servanthood. And they'll take some time to pull together as a team.

You'll have a trip, but not a maximized mission experience. For every moment you spend in preparation, you'll get many more back that make your trip the most it can be.

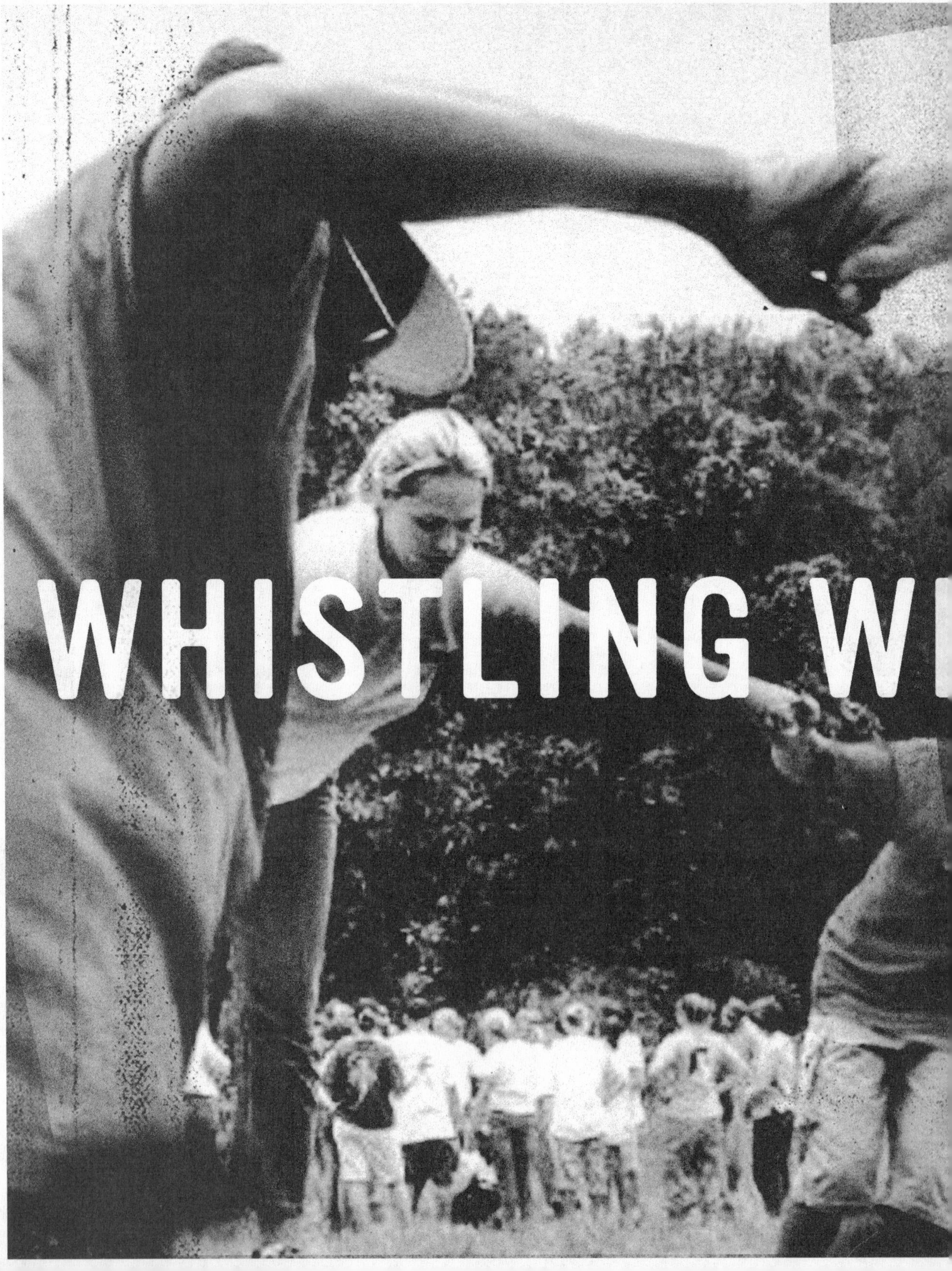

WHISTLING W

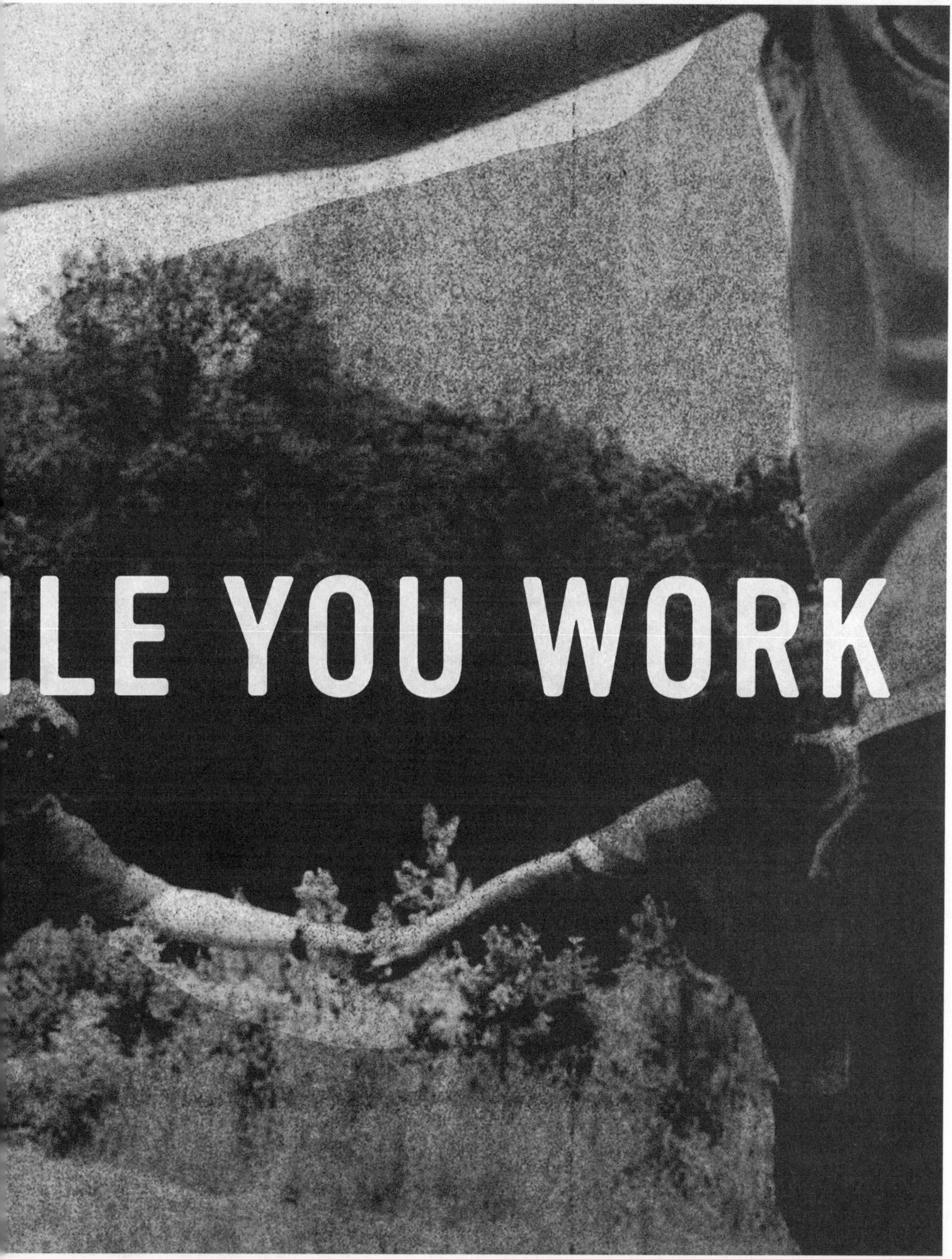
ILE YOU WORK

CH. 5

WHISTLING WHILE YOU WORK

It's all but inevitable. You're on your mission project, challenging your team to push hard. To do their best. To go beyond what they ever dreamed they were capable of.

There's an enormous chance your students will startle you with their willingness and ability to do great things with God.

Nevertheless, there's an equally enormous chance that the project, which once sounded great, will feel impossibly hard. Suddenly the trip isn't so fun anymore—pounding one more nail, singing one more song, performing one more play, knocking on one more door to pass out a Bible, enduring one more wimpy, lukewarm shower feel impossible. So your group starts to spit more nails than they pound. Every kid thinks every other kid has a better job. You're stabbed with the words, "I thought you said this would be fun."

That's feedback. It could be the kind of whiney complaining that unravels a trip or it might provide you with valid information.

The hardest part of any mission trip isn't getting there. It's pulling off whatever you came to do. Along the way you can expect your pack of students to act like the Seven Dwarves. You can count on some being perpetually happy no matter what the circumstances. A few will be bashful. But some will be sleepy, sneezy, grumpy, or dopey. You can even count on a big-brained doc showing up.

You'd like your team members to whistle while they work. Well, maybe that's a bit much. But when your students don't perform the way you had hoped, it's easy to go negative—to hurl a verbal barrage that you're in charge of a bunch of brats. It's easy to let your expectations slide—after all, youth only want entertainment, all students are slackers, today's adolescents are all so shallow they can't work.

The success of your trip depends on keeping your students—and yourself—motivated and moving in the right direction.

When you really want to know how your trip is going, stay calm and ask yourself two questions:

QUESTION 1: ARE WE MEETING OUR GOALS FOR THE PROJECT?

When you're off on a trip and things don't exactly go as you envisioned, you might be facing a genuine reason to be upset. Or you might just be having a bad day. Consider the fact that feelings seldom accurately measure how ministry is going when you're back home. They're even less reliable when you're in the emotional jumble of a mission trip. You can feel like your project is progressing incredibly well but in reality not be accomplishing anything, or you can feel ready to hang it up and be on the edge of a breakthrough.

The only way you can measure whether you're making real progress is to step back, stay sane, and quiz yourself and your team about whether you're meeting the goals you set for the trip. You might have a long list of specific objectives you're aiming at, so revisit those. But here are some simple questions that get at the big three goals to be accomplished on any good trip:

+ ARE YOUR YOUTH GROWING? Your youth might be growing closer to Jesus—or growing resentful. Mission projects often involve sacrifice, but students should sacrifice willingly. Are they working out of a love for Jesus and compassion for people or are they feeling used and manipulated, as if leaders have lashed a gigantic cross on them?

+ ARE OTHERS BENEFITING? It can be hard to be brutally honest, but ask yourself: What concrete results—spiritual, physical, mental, and emotional—do we have to show for the time, energy, and money we've invested?

+ IS GOD BEING GLORIFIED? God isn't only interested in the results you get. He wants you to get results in the right way. He's wondering this: Are people seeing Me in what you do?

No trip is perfect. But you'd probably agree that your trip is not going as planned if you're not seeing growth in your youth, good being done to others, and God being glorified. If you see progress in the big three goals, you have reason to say thanks to God, to pat your group on the shoulder, and to kick back with some coconut milk.

QUESTION 2: ARE YOU CARING FOR THE GROUP IN A WAY THAT YOU CAN MEET THE GOALS?

You'll only be able to meet your project goals if students are cared for in a way that helps them have what it takes to minister day after day. And the biggest way their needs are met—apart from God supernaturally zapping them, which he does—is by you and the adult leaders pressing forward as their loving leaders.

Lots of folks with a passion for missions and service have a bent toward doing incredibly hard things for God. They expect the best of themselves and have the same high expectations of their youth.

If that's you, you might be drawing your inspiration from Jesus, the one who endured the cross (Hebrews 12:2). That's a dream-casting, goal-grabbing, biblical attitude. It's what Oswald Chambers was describing when he wrote that Christians are to be like Christ, "broken bread" and "poured out wine." The apostle Paul tells us that as Christians we're appointed to suffer (Philippians 1:29) and rattles off a list of all the things he endured to pursue God's will (2 Corinthians 11:16-33). Add to that the fact that it's hard to think about meeting your own needs or coddling your students when you're face to face with poverty or spiritual darkness. You want to go for broke. How can you offer anything less than your absolute best to the Lord who died for you—and for a world that is hurting?

But get this: Jesus didn't jump right to the cross, and his followers didn't go directly to the dungeons. Both Jesus and Paul took time to enjoy God's creation, God's people, and God himself. Jesus modeled hard work for his disciples (Mark 16:20). He urged them to try again so he could bless their efforts (Luke 5:4-5). He also told them to come away and rest with him (Mark 6:31). Paul knew how to enjoy good things as a gift from God (1 Timothy 4:4).

You can't expect your students to survive with any less care than Jesus or Paul needed. So study your students, both when they're working like dogs and when they're dogging it. What do they need from you?

Bottom line: Your job is to make the trip sustainable. Better yet, you can try to make it a joy.

KEEPING YOUR TEAM MOVING

Here are 10 big hints about caring for your trip participants to keep your team together and on task.

1. KEEP LEADERS ON TRACK.

Few teams stage a total mutiny. But when students start to drag or complain, the first place to look isn't at the failings of your students. Look first at your adult leaders. No, adults aren't responsible for the mysterious inner mechanisms of the adolescent mind and its tendency to form its own opinions—good, bad, or ugly—and to act accordingly. Yet there's always a question to ask: Are your youth in any way reflecting adult leader attitudes?

Yikes!

If trip leaders ain't happy, ain't nobody happy. If leaders are dumping on kids, the kids aren't going to do well. If leaders aren't doing their utmost to model good attitudes and actions, most youth will follow suit.

Here's how leaders can stay ahead of the pack to help your youth do their best as followers:

✚ *Be the leader.* You have a choice: Be your youth's buddy or be their leader. You can't have it both ways. When you doubt that, remember your role. You're in charge, and you're the adult.

✚ *Stay motivated.* You might be the one who needs an attitude adjustment. Do you need some time alone? Is there a problem you need to confront? What do you or your fellow leaders need to stay positive?

✚ *Get support.* No person leads a team alone, and your team's adults can't be supportive if they don't get into each other's worlds. Spend time daily checking in with each other and praying for the project.

✚ *Set the pace.* Youth take their cues from you. How hard are you—the key leader—working at your tasks? How much do your students see you in there with them sweating, knocking on doors, or singing your lungs out? Students understand if you have multiple working groups to coordinate, but if they only see you socializing and snapping pictures, they'll want to do the same. When you use your presence to model faithful work, your youth will follow—and that will do your heart good.

✚ *Squash chaos.* Anarchy rattles most adults. Few youth want a situation that feels out of control. If students are acting out because they don't know where the behavior boundaries are—or because boundaries aren't consistently enforced—you're creating an environment where students can't thrive. And even though confronting youth isn't much fun, in the long run you're making life miserable for yourself and everyone else if you don't put a lid on misbehavior.

✚ *Stick together.* Just as kids often play parents against each other, trip participants can try to pit one leader against another. If you sense your leadership team isn't all on the same page—concerning workload, time off, rules, expectations—don't let the problem go. Talk. If you're not together and on task, your youth won't be either.

2. KEEP TALKING.

You're on the trip—and you want your team members to do the right thing, like whatever you flew halfway around the world to do. Yet you've come to an impasse. Some of your youth seem walled up inside, unresponsive to your leadership.

You can work on your students from the outside—using a threat or a bribe. Or you can work on them from the inside by injecting new, better thoughts into their heads.

You do that by talking with students, not at them. Your abilities to listen well and speak wisely are your greatest tools for leading your team. Whether you've run into a problem or just want your group to stay on course, keep up the dialogue.

✚ *Listen.* If your students have problems or complaints, give them a chance to talk. Ask them for a solution they think will work. Help them ponder the consequences of their proposal. Then keep a dialogue going so they embrace a positive choice of their own accord. Explosions happen when youth aren't heard, and mutinies happen when they feel manipulated.

✚ *Expect the best.* Youth live up or down to expectations. Catch your students doing good and applaud their hard work.

✚ *Stay positive.* There might be times when you need to say tough things and confront attitudes or actions that shouldn't be happening. But if you yell, you've already lost. Save your loud mouth for circumstances when someone is in immediate bodily danger.

✚ *Blast to your past.* Counting to 10 might not help you be compassionate and kind, but it might help to ask yourself: How would you have acted in this situation at that age? More importantly, what did it take to move you to a different point of view or a different set of actions?

✚ *Take a time out.* When things don't go well, slow down. Whether you need to pull aside an individual, a small group, or the whole team, don't just try to wish a problem away. Work it out.

✚ *Remember your goals.* You need to chat with your team daily about things you discussed during preparation sessions—your goals, how the trip might be hard, the rewards you would get. Set your goals in front of your group at the start of every day.

+ *Challenge by choice.* Any phys ed teacher knows you can put a pack of students on a track, but you can't make them run. You can, however, challenge and encourage them. Tell them that you can't force them to do their best. But you're asking them to. Let them choose to take up the challenge.

+ *Tell them where they're at.* Smart athletes pace themselves according to where they are in a race. Do your students a favor by giving them a sense of where they're at in their project. Start the day by patting them on the back for whatever progress they've made. Remind them what they'll do that day. And throughout the day let them know how far them are from the finish line—how much time is left to work that day. Like a good coach, encourage them to sprint to the end.

+ *Process the experience.* At the close of each day, take 15 to 20 minutes to talk about how the day went. Is someone sick? Hurting? Are things going especially well? If your group is too big for everyone to have a chance to talk, break into small groups for part of the time. Rule for adult leaders: Listen before you talk.

3. KEEP A SCHEDULE.

You've got tons to do. If you want to do your task—do it well—and have enough time for meals, clean up, processing, relaxation, teaching, and worship, you've got to keep things moving. Some schedule tips:

+ *Set your schedule ahead of time.* Making a schedule up as you go along will drive at least half your youth crazy. So think it through, put it on paper, post it each day, and adjust it as necessary. At the end of the day, ask yourself whether your students were dying or whether they were able to work hard to the end, tired but satisfied.

+ *Know when to quit.* Listen to your hosts, but here are some guidelines: Putting in two or three hours doesn't stretch your youth and doesn't accomplish squat. Most students can handle a workday of five to eight hours if they experience a little variety in their tasks. Putting in more than eight hours is pushing beyond what adults happily do. That's why it's called overtime.

+ *Take breaks.* You might be a frenzied maniac in your work habits. Just because you don't need a break doesn't mean your students don't need one. For quite a few of your youth, your trip is the first formal, extended work experience they've ever had. After a couple of hours—maybe before—they'll need a few minutes to regroup, whether they've been doing rump-busting labor or playing checkers and chatting with senior citizens.

+ *Plan surprises.* Keep an eye on your youth, and when they're pooping out, break out the refreshments. Bring them surprise sodas and junk food as a treat—that's especially appropriate in the middle of an afternoon toward the end of the week. Teach them the adult art of taking a break and getting back to work.

+ *Make time for clean up.* Whether it's putting away tools or tracts, you'll ultimately save time and frustration by having everything back in place, ready to go the next day.

+ *Don't mess with free time.* Some youth don't mind if you plan every minute of their day. Most do. When your team members' whole existence revolves around doing what they're supposed to when they're supposed to, they need down time. If a workday unavoidably runs long, compensate by shortening the next day's work. Do the math and tell them your plan as soon as possible.

4. KEEP THINGS FAIR.

Face it. Some tasks on a mission trip look way more fun than others. And it doesn't cut it to say, "Life isn't fair," when your youth notice. If you don't make a reasonable effort to keep rights, privileges, and hardships equitable, your youth will smell a cop-out. You'll be setting up an antagonistic relationship with your students that you don't want to have to deal with. Some ways to keep things as fair as possible:

+ *Rotate jobs.* If you can rotate youth between different work assignments, great. If rotating students in and out of a setting will ruin the flow of the work they're trying to accomplish, tell them that. But still do whatever else you can to keep it even.

+ *Give every one a taste.* Of the really nasty jobs, that is. Everyone cooks. Everyone pulls dish duty. Everyone gets a turn swabbing down the bathrooms. And everyone helps pick up at the end of your trip.

+ *Play by one set of rules.* If you let favorite youth—or adult leaders—have privileges out of line with the rules and privileges set up for everyone else, you'll destroy team unity.

+ *Let kids lead.* Letting your more mature students set the pace for tasks helps many students fall in line. While you'd like to count on the older ones, sometimes your younger students are the more mature ones.

+ *Challenge by choice.* When there's no way around a hard or unfair job, admit it. Ask for volunteers. Some students always want to tackle the worst. Your job is to make sure they don't overdo it—and to not make the rest of the group feel guilty for not being heroic.

+ *Buddy up.* Students deserve a buddy to work with until they prove otherwise. Friends can prod friends to work hard in a way you never can. When one moans, for example, put the other "in charge" of that person for a while. Make it their job to cheer the friend on and model diligence.

+ *Don't make kids work alone.* Not even as a consequence for rotten behavior. If you have a youth who won't get with the program, you're better off pairing him or her with an adult leader—not as punishment, but to help set the pace through encouragement.

+ *Don't let kids work alone.* If a student says she prefers to work alone, you can give her an individual kind of task, but don't let her work apart from the group. It doesn't usually turn out well.

+ *Point out the fun side of what they're doing and the down side of what they're not.* To a girl who's pouring concrete, hanging out with little kids might look sweet. Reminding her, for example, that she really doesn't like taking care of her own little siblings brings some reality to the situation.

5. KEEP CLEAN.

You don't have to be doing demolition to wind up sweaty and dirty. And one of the beautiful aspects of mission trips is that everyone learns there's more to life than being beautiful.

But one of the best ways to regain sanity is to get clean. It's not just a matter of comfort but of health and hygiene. A shower a day keeps away wicked cases of jungle rot that likes to grow in dark places.

You're probably not expecting clean-up facilities to be luxurious, but it helps to mentally brace for the worst. Showers might not even be at the location where you bunk. At least one large hosting group houses students in churches and elementary schools and deliberately uses off-site showers—at YMCAs and community centers—to limit the amount of time spent grooming. Smart move, but maybe not what you expected.

Here are some noncruel guidelines for getting clean:

+ *Downplay getting primped.* You want students to feel clean and presentable. But they don't need to be their gussied-up best. You can exercise some control over that by banning large make-up kits as well as electric goodies like hair dryers and curling irons.

+ *Limit shower hours.* If you get everyone in and out of the showers in one defined time period, you'll keep your group from spending unlimited hours on routine personal maintenance. You'll save time for other good things.

+ *Clean up at the end of the day.* Whether you're building houses or knocking on doors, clean up after a hard day of work. As a bonus, students get to be clean for evening activities when they probably care most about looking good—and they sleep better. For most projects participants can look a little rumpled in the morning.

+ *Invest in shower shoes.* Aqua socks, sandals, or flip-flops help you brave the nastiest shower facilities.

+ *Be good to God's earth.* If you'll be scrubbing up in a lake, river, or other natural body of water, pack biodegradable soap and shampoo.

6. KEEP UP THE FUN.

Don't expect to hear the exact words, "Are we having fun yet?" But that doesn't mean your youth aren't wondering where all the fun went. Again, in a hard-core setting like a short-term mission trip, it doesn't hurt to remember that our God is a God of green pastures and still waters. If that's where God is leading them, here's how to stay at the head of the pack.

+ *Talk up "a different kind of fun."* You're experiencing a kind of fun found in few other activities. You get to hang out with each other 24/7. You get the satisfaction of hard work. You're growing spiritually. It might not be the stomach-churning thrill of a roller coaster, but it's a fun that can't be beat.

+ *Get out and about.* You didn't drive to Appalachia to keep your nose three inches from the board you're scraping. Meet the locals. Find out what life is like where you are.

+ *Make work fun.* Talk. Sing. Make tough tasks a game or a contest to finish.

+ *Take time off each day.* You're going to take time to work, clean, eat, talk, and worship. Each of those activities can feel like work for youth—so you still need a limited amount of totally unstructured free time. To the extent that you have input into the schedule, plan for half-hour blocks of free time after breakfast, after lunch, and after supper, with another 45 minutes to an hour before lights out.

+ *Take a day off each week.* It might seem bluntly obvious that your group needs time off on extended trips, but on mission trips, a go-for-it attitude often creeps in that says you can't afford to take time off. With chores like laundering clothes on Saturday and participating in worship services on Sunday, students are taxed. Take time for sightseeing, unstructured time off, group games—whatever your group is up for.

+ *Eat the food.* If you're tripping to a foreign country, you no doubt know that eating the wrong stuff and getting sick is zero fun. So is never tasting the local food. Check out the rules for eating in Chapter 3 for staying healthy.

+ *Buy souvenirs.* You might not be into knick-knacks, pennants, key chains, or coconut monkey heads. But if you're working in an area that's unlike home, make sure team members get a chance to pick up mementos.

+ Keep a lid on pranks. The dictionary describes a prank as "a mischievous trick or silly stunt done for amusement." The problem is not only that the humor comes at someone else's expense, but also that the humor often doesn't translate well in mission settings. Leave that brand of amusement at home.

7. FEED YOUR STUDENTS SPIRITUALLY.

Remember? A mission trip is how Jesus trained his disciples. He gave them preparation beforehand and he did follow-up afterwards. But he also made time for on-the-go teaching.

If your students have the energy to stay alert through an hourong lecture each day, you might not be working them hard enough. A load of ways to build content into your days:

+ *Start your day with devotions.* Giving students 15 to 30 minutes for a "quiet time" each morning not only conveys biblical encouragement each day but also could start a lifelong habit of spiritual growth. Are you wondering what your youth should read? Get each team member a copy of the devotional in this kit, *Mission Trip Prep: A Student Journal for Capturing the Experience.*

+ *Memorize the Word.* Help your students hang onto God's promises by requiring them to memorize a verse each day or two. Pick your own or use the student journal to guide you.

+ *Meet other Christians.* Let God teach your youth through other Christians in the locale where you're working—missionaries, local pastors, people-in-the-pew. If you're contributing physical labor, it's especially important to put faces with the ministry you're doing.

+ *Remember why you're working.* The connection between swinging a hammer and majestic spiritual goals might be hard for youth to see. Employ their imaginations to see how you're meeting your goals of their growth, people's good, and God's glory. If you're rehabbing an unoccupied house, for example, challenge your students to imagine who will live there when you're done. If you're fixing an empty school, talk about the students who will attend.

+ *Pray often.* You don't have to pray longwinded prayers for your youth to realize that prayer undergirds every task of the day. Pray a lot. Model bringing little issues to God in prayer.

+ *Worship.* Worship connects you to each other and to the God who sent you on this wacky trip. It's indispensable.

+ *Regroup in the evenings.* Take time each night to meet for worship, prayer, stupid skits, encouragement, sharing highs and lows of the day, celebrating the good that's happened, and hanging out together. It might work best to spread the excitement of the positives as one large group and to deal with the challenges and tough stuff in groups of five or six. If you're participating with multiple churches, make sure you take time to meet with your own students each evening to catch up on the day.

+ *Hit them between the eyes.* Whatever you're teaching, make it short, sweet, and to the point. Your students are likely to be more spiritually receptive and more sleepy than they are at home.

8. KEEP STRONG.

No one has a their mother on the trip—well, maybe one or two whose mom came with as a chaperone. While your youth need to take responsibility for self-care, you can set some boundaries that help:

+ *Make time to sleep.* You might have done retreats or camps where students go nonstop with hardly any sleep. Most mission trips are different, with youth wanting badly to sleep after long days of work. It's not hard to make sure your students can get eight solid hours of sleep—lights out at 11, up at seven, breakfast at half-past seven. If you're driving to your site and have the cargo capacity, it's worth hauling inflatable mattresses and, depending on the weather and your housing, some monster fans.

✝ *Give them adequate food, snacks, and water.* When the disciples complained about lunch, Jesus fed them. If the person cooking for you scrimps or has no idea how much working, growing kids actually eat, speak up. Or make a grocery run so you can enlarge the meal or make reasonably healthy snacks available. If you're working in hot or humid weather, make sure water is always handy and that students are drinking. Sounds basic—until someone doesn't drink and gets deathly sick.

✝ *Make sure your youth eat—and eat well.* Many adolescents are like vacuum cleaners, inhaling every scrap of food in sight. Others teeter on the edge of starvation as they struggle with eating disorders. Keep an eye on what youth eat—too much junk or too few calories. While it's not your job to monitor every mouthful, it becomes your problem when a student is too wired or weak.

✝ *Respect privacy.* When you're living close on a mission trip, you'll find out more about students than you want to know. You might have middle schoolers who can't sleep without their stuffed animal or ragged blanket. You might have a student sobbing in the middle of the night about problems at home that most of us can't begin to fathom. You might discover a number of kids who need bedwetting medicine. Be discreet with what you know. The whole team doesn't need to find out that a girl has menstrual cramps or that a guy with a stomachache has trotted to the bathroom 14 times this morning. As a leader it's your job to zip your lips about issues the group has no right or need to know about.

9. KEEP SAFE.

Good news: Mission trips almost always attract the best of youth—and bring out the best in them. That doesn't mean everything will always run smoothly. Here are some huge ways you can keep your students safe:

✝ *Watch your back.* No matter where you go, your group is going to look like out-of-towners at best, rich gringos at worst. It's hard to describe how a trip can be undone if you're robbed or become victims of violence. Listen to and follow any tips your hosts give you on being street smart.

✝ *Keep tools at the work site.* Tools aren't toys. It's surprising how quickly a paint scraper in the hands of a youth becomes a ninja weapon or a screwdriver becomes a dart.

+ *Maintain guy-girl boundaries.* Pairing off can put a huge crimp on the tasks at hand—so much so that some groups ban it.

Another guy-girl biggie: Think of how the most conservative person in your church would evaluate your sleeping arrangements—then double that amount of concern—and ask yourself these questions:

+ Are guys and girls adequately separated?
+ Are changing areas sufficiently private?
+ Is the trip turning into a giant pajama party?

+ *Control contraband.* Your pretrip discussions probably persuaded most students to leave anything you've banned at home. Don't make a scene if you need to take something away. Unless it's illegal, just ask for it and put it away until the end of the trip.

If your students do bring along something illegal—drugs, for example—or are somehow involved in other criminal activity on the trip, have you thought about how you will deal with it? What policy would your church expect you to enforce if you were back home? Do they want you to talk to parents or to police? In cases such as sexual abuse, your state might deem you or some other adult leader a mandatory reporter, which requires you to report the situation to government authorities.

Be psychologically prepared to see a student cuffed if circumstances warrant it—to save the reputation of God and the rest of your group. In other cases of outright illegal behavior, sending the offending student home seems to be the minimum action you should take.

+ *Don't waste.* Throwing away food and wasting work materials don't go over well with nonaffluent locals or missions staff living on modest salaries.

+ *Make consequences fit the crime.* Whether you're faced with blatant rebellion or something less threatening——like students going AWOL for large quantities of Mountain Dew—use logical consequences to enforce your rules. If students throw food, make them cook. If they blow fire extinguishers, make them clean up and pay for recharges. If they keep other students awake, send the offending students off to their sleeping bags early the next night. Again, don't make a scene. And especially don't make idle threats. Just enforce the rules.

+ *Expect your youth to use common sense.* You don't need to make a rule for everything. Some behaviors are bad enough that they need correction right away— the first time they happen, no warnings need to be given before a consequence occurs.

+ *Send a student home.* What behavior is bad enough to merit the ultimate mission trip punishment? Start with the obvious:

  + Anything seriously illegal—as in, "If a police officer had seen that, you'd be in jail."
  + Anything seriously dangerous—like brandishing an eight-inch knife or using a wrist rocket to slingshot stones at other students.
  + Anything seriously rebellious—like stuff that will rip a team apart or cause your hosts or local people to dismiss your efforts.

10. KEEP YOUR LIFELINES OPEN.

You aren't taking this trip alone. Sure, you probably remember that you have an adult or two or more with you, but you also have a support network back home.

+ *Deal with homesickness.* You might have youth relieved to get away from home. You could have others who cry themselves to sleep each night because they miss their moms and dads. Set guidelines for phone calls home—when and how long.

+ *Write letters.* If you're gone much more than a week, require a letter home—one per week from each participant. Not to a friend, but to parents or legal guardians. Even if you beat your letters home, letters demonstrate that you didn't forget the people who made the trip possible.

+ Know what to say. If you have to call parents about a sick or injured youth and don't know what to say, have this starter phrase handy: "I need to tell you something about (name)." Then describe as briefly as possible:

  + The current situation
  + What you're doing to solve the problem.

Then you can describe all the other details.

+ *Communicate with your church.* A call or e-mail every few days to your home church or parachurch organization keeps you on the prayer chain. If a major incident happens to your group, keep your pastor or other designated contact informed.

Know where to get help. If you're at a location where dialing 9-1-1 isn't the obvious answer, ask your host how to get medical help for both injuries and illnesses—shortly after your arrival. Find out how to get emergency assistance. Plan for a situation in which you need to get help and every second counts. Don't rely on someone else to know how to get in touch with police, a fire crew, or an ambulance.

PULLING IT ALL TOGETHER

Keeping your group on track involves finding the right pressure point between pushing hard and slowing down. It's a lot like learning to drive a car. If you're cautious and never edge up to the speed limit, you're in for a slow ride. But if you start taking twists and turns too fast, you might slide off the road or have close brushes where you cause other cars to collide. You might glance in your rearview mirror and discover a body you ran over while you weren't paying attention.

In leading your students, there's a time to stomp on the gas and a time to apply the brakes. If you stay alert to the condition of your students, you'll know what you need to do when.

CH. 6

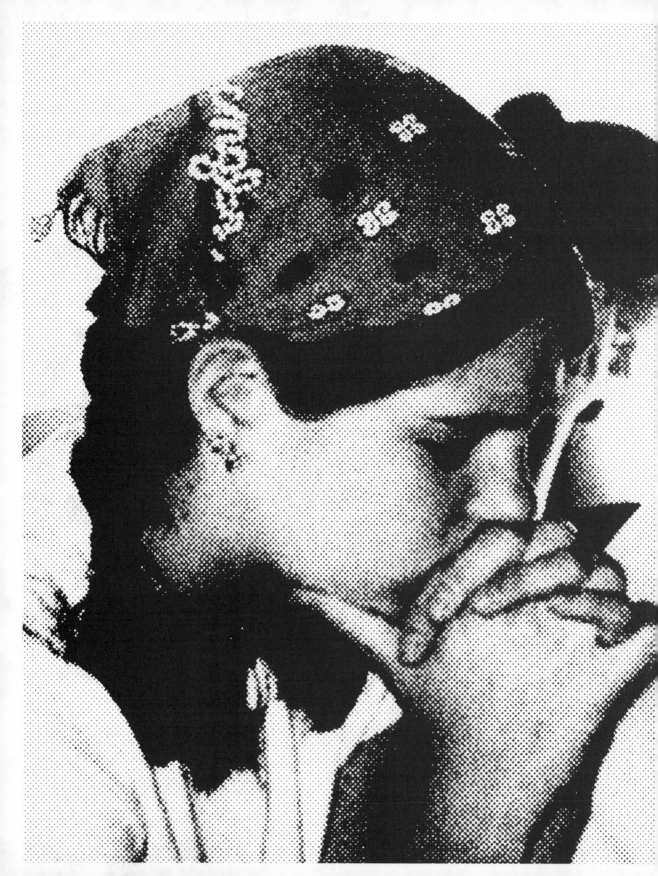

MAKING THE TRIP STICK

CH. 6

MAKING THE TRIP STICK

You're so relieved to be home after your mission project that you barely notice that everyone has ditched you and left you to unload the vans alone. Post-trip, everyone smiles. Over the next few days a mom calls you and says, "Abby had a great time. It's like she's glowing." A dad grabs you in church and tells you, "Chris couldn't stop talking about everything y'all did." And a couple weeks later you get a thank you note in the mail that gushes, "It sounds like you had a real adventure. It's made such a difference in Jade's spiritual life."

But after a month or two you hear rumblings. People don't have the heart to break you the truth when they know you dripped sweat to assure the mission project succeeded. But parents mumble loud enough for you to hear: "That trip didn't make any difference in the kids' lives when they came home. Rachel still won't listen, and she still tortures her little sister."

You can't control everything that youth learn or don't learn on your project. You can't fix everything in a few short days or weeks together. You can't dictate what leaks out of students' brains when they get home. But one thing is for sure. You want one singular result from all the work you pour into a mission project: for participants to take the trip home.

When you've taken a group on an experience that cultivates their growth, makes a dent in evil, and brings praise to God, nothing feels worse than figuring out a month or a year later that it made squat difference in daily life. And few of the criticisms of short-term missions have as much truth as "projects don't make a long-term difference in the lives of youth." You can counter those objections—and serve your students well—by getting a grip on your group's post-trip experience.

MULTIPLYING OPPORTUNITIES

The little-known secret of short-term missions is that the biggest challenge isn't getting ready to go or even handling the project once you're there. It's making the connection between your project and real life once you get home.

Guess what? Your trip isn't over when you pull into the church parking lot. You have two jobs left. One is easy: Celebrate what you've done.

The other takes more effort: Make the project stick. Chapters 11 and 12 contain ideas for two follow-up sessions to get you started. But for now, think broadly about what your youth will need when they hit home.

Your goal is to figure out whatever made your trip rock for God—and then do more of it. It isn't tough to spot some of the key components that make a mission trip mean something to your students. Your students might experience Christian community like never before. They likely will catch a glimpse of God's work in the world. The minute they get home, they'll probably be itching to go back—or go somewhere for God. And they might be driven to keep making a practical difference in their world.

You want a package of opportunities ready when you return home that will help trip members stay engaged. They're the same opportunities that will fire the enthusiasm of other youth in your group. If you want to keep the lessons learned on your trip alive, give your team members four flavors of ongoing activities:

+ *More community*—chances to continue building deep relationships with other youth who are passionate about God.

+ *More vision*—teaching to open their eyes to God's global activities.

+ *More missions*—plans for future mission trips, including increasing challenges.

+ *More service*—opportunities to serve right here and right now.

If you can put those four pieces in place, you have a plan that will keep your work from wasting away. Take a look now at what the key pieces look like.

KEY ONE: ONGOING COMMUNITY

Your trip might grow out of a well-established youth program. Or it might plant seeds that sprout into a real youth group for the first time.

Either way, a mission project is often the first time youth connect with other Christians in the deep community they've read about in the Bible. They gather around service, not just socializing. They get to know God as well as each other. And they may have figured out that depending on other Christians is the only way they'll fully mature or change the world.

It's not enough to say, "Well, they'll come back to our church and fit right in." There are a couple things that need to happen to make the most of the relationships they built:

+ YOU WANT TO SPREAD THE FIRE TO YOUTH WHO STAYED BEHIND. Students care about whether you liked the projects—sort of. The real authorities regarding the coolness of your trip, however, are your team members. Other youth will naturally catch the enthusiasm of your team, with one exception: You and the team can't make nonparticipants feel like losers.

You'll want to share what you did—why you went, what you accomplished, how great it was. But don't judge students as spiritually slow for not going on your project. There are a thousand reasons they might not have gone, reasons you might never know, reasons that play just great with God. And don't make a clique out of your mission team.

+ YOU WANT TO KEEP THE BONDS BUILT DURING THE PROJECT BURNING. You can start by finding out what your youth want to do to stay connected and committed—like when they want to meet, whether they want to party or pray—and doing it. Coming home from a mission trip is like high school commencement. No, it won't ever be the same. No, not everyone will make it to every follow-up meeting. But for those who want it, you can cultivate the same spirit your youth felt on the project.

The follow-up sessions in Chapters 11 and 12 give you two structured meeting times to talk about sharing what you learned and to reassemble as a team. But for now, jot down some of your own ideas:

How can our group stay glued together when they arrive home? What opportunities already exist for team members to stay connected?

_____

_____

What's the best way the group can pass on what they've learned to the rest of our group?

_____

_____

What will our trip participants need to feel acknowledged and appreciated by the bulk of our church?

_____

_____

KEY 2: ONGOING FEEDING

Most mission trips are so packed with activity and practical discipleship that there's not much time for teaching much content about missions—so that even students who have been on multiple short-term mission projects might not have thought much about God's big-picture work around the world. On most projects what participants learn is local compassion. That's fantastic. But you can fill out their experience and start them thinking explosively about their lifetime involvement in ministry by giving them a global vision.

Once you're home, students are primed to learn. Now you have time to process the experience. So round out the content. Remind them why they went. And coach them into a long-term commitment to God's global cause.

The landscape of worldwide missions changes rapidly. But you can educate your youth in four areas crucial to God's work in the world:

GLOBAL OUTREACH

You can pile on the facts and history of world missions high and deep until your youth qualify for doctorates, but here are a couple of facts students need to understand about the spiritual neediness of the world:

+ Missions experts estimate that about 20 percent of the world's population hasn't heard enough about Christ to have a real opportunity to decide for or against him. That's well over a billion people.

+ These "least-reached peoples" fall into five big groups—followers of Hinduism, Islam, Buddhism, and tribal religions, as well as the ethnic Chinese, who as a whole have traditionally adhered to a mixture of Confucianism, Buddhism, ancestor veneration, and other Asian belief systems. Most live in a band that crosses Africa and Asia between the 10th and 40th north latitude—the 10/40 Window.

The unreached cultural groups that reside within this region are at the center of strategic missions activities, and students who want to cultivate a global vision will want to begin by learning about outreach among these peoples. For starters, point them to www.1040window.org and www.acmc.org.

THE PERSECUTED CHURCH

Your students care about way more than shopping malls and video games—if you give them something important to care about, that is. And here's something to care about: More Christians have died for their faith in the 20th century than in the previous 19 centuries combined. Millions of Christians around the world suffer rape, political repression, imprisonment, torture, harassment, discrimination, and family division because of their faith. Children of believers are sold into slavery for the cost of a CD. Every 3 1/2 minutes a Christian dies for the faith. Do the math: During a typical one-hour youth group meeting, 17 Christians will be martyred somewhere in the world.

You can pry open the eyes of your youth to worldwide persecution of Christians. They'll meet people who might not look like them yet worship the same Jesus—and suffer for it. The quickest way to get a handle on the issue is the curriculum *Student Underground* (Youth Specialties, 2000). The package works as a high-impact retreat, a lock-in event, or spread out over four weekly sessions. However you use the package, your group will understand the situation of suffering sisters and brothers, hear why to care, and discover real ways to aid the persecuted church—and keep their missions vision alive.

WORLD HUNGER

Hunger, disease, homelessness, and violence against street kids—involvement in these big world issues is another means for making your trip stick. If you've never tackled these issues as a group, start by involving your whole group in World Vision's 30-Hour Famine, a youth-oriented hunger fundraiser. The 30-Hour Famine is an annual worldwide event that involves thousands of groups from junior high age on up in a learning and service weekend. As youth experience hunger firsthand, they not only gain insights into world needs but also have the opportunity to stretch their understanding of God's goals for their lives. Find complete instructions at www.30hourfamine.org.

Organizations like World Vision (www.worldvision.org), Compassion International (www.compassion.com), and Bread for the World (www.bread.org) can provide information on sponsoring children and other year-around activities to fight hunger, bring practical help to the poor, and engage in local, national, and international social action.

EVANGELISM TRAINING

The idea of traditional witnessing is enough to terrify any youth group, even students headed off on a mission project. It might even scare you. But learning to share the Good News about Jesus in an engaging way isn't impossible. *Live the Life!* is a video-driven training kit (Youth Specialties, 1998) designed to help you equip students to share their faith at home or on a project. The series includes videos, a leader's guide, and student workbooks that will grow your students' confidence as they learn to reach out to others in honesty and love.

Looking to make a bigger commitment to equipping your students to reach out? Plug them into DC/LA—a five-day, once-every-three-years summer experience that helps students learn to tell God's story to the people they love. Using interactive learning wrapped in worship, fun, and peer-to-peer sharing, this youth evangelism training conference has equipped more than 90,000 students since 1985. Find out more at www.dcla2003.org or www.yfc.org.

And for yet another option, check out SEMP (Students Equipped to Minister to Peers) from SonLife (www.sonlife.com). At week-long conferences held throughout the U.S. and Canada and around the world, SEMP assists you and your high school students in developing a real-life plan for reaching friends. A similar program, EQUIP, helps junior high students grow, care, and share.

Of these four key areas, which would most catch my group's interest?

KEY 3: ONGOING MISSIONS

You might be the kind of person who starts mulling during one vacation what you want to do on the next. You pull out an atlas or stop by a bookstore for travel books—you know, to fend off ugly feelings of having to reenter reality. Whether you're wired that way or not, you can bet that in the midst of any mission project, you'll have students wondering what they get to do next time. And rather than letting that visionary enthusiasm wane, harness it. Stay one step ahead.

Your goal isn't to turn every youth who takes part in your trip into a career missionary. If you're thinking big-picture, however, one of your goals is to permanently connect them to God's cause. You can help them make a reasoned, lasting commitment to some form of missions involvement. You can help them find their own key role—going themselves, giving financial support, mobilizing others to go or give, or praying.

Many students ache to take another trip. And lots of them look for increasing challenges. The most effective youth mission programs map out a progression of trips. A long-term picture for a church might look like this: You provide at-church and in-town service projects for younger kids and families. You offer nearby projects for middle schoolers and rookie high schoolers. You might choose to reserve out-of-state and overseas mission projects for seasoned high schoolers. You can also challenge ultramature students to take extended trips with organizations that cater to individuals.

The point is to engage as many students as possible while they are young, interested, and free from summer job conflicts—and to give all students the privilege of increased responsibility to look forward to as they grow older.

As you dream about an overarching plan for your youth, you can think of possible trips in terms of a progression of challenges, like the three tiers of outreaches laid out by the host group Adventures in Missions:

LEVEL 1

Objective: Provide tools for growth.

Description: One week, low-risk ministry environment, semi-comfortable housing.

Requirements: Participants have accepted Jesus as Savior, are able to verbalize one's testimony and to share a simple Gospel message.

LEVEL 2

Objective: Focus on listening, prayer, and sharing Christ through relationships with the local people.

Description: 7-14 days, medium-intensity ministry environment. Leaders committed to stretching their students.

Requirements: Same as level 1, plus prior ministry experience.

LEVEL 3

Objective: Serve radically, allowing God to lead on a daily basis.

Description: 10-14 days, high-intensity ministry environment. Students engage in relational, evangelistic ministries almost the entire time.

Requirements: Same as Level 2, plus greater maturity and experience in allowing God to lead.

All along the way you want to look for projects that comfortably fit your group. Yet without some amount of stretching you won't see growth. One caution: Don't announce what you can't produce or maintain or think you might change. But it's great to dream and, as plans solidify, to map out for your students what they can look forward to while they're in your group.

So what's our next gig? What do I dream of doing next?

_____

_____

What do my students want to do next? What might keep them enthused about missions?

_____

_____

_____

What do parents want?

_____

_____

How will the leaders from this trip react to my plan? What do they want to do?

_____

_____

KEY 4: ONGOING SERVICE

When you've taken a group on a short-term mission project, you've cracked the nut. You've done the hard thing. You've given your youth a taste of sacrificial service. Assuming they had any amount of fun in the process, they're probably already thinking not just about jamming on another mission trip but finding ways to serve at home.

You might already have created opportunities for community. You might be teaching your youth about missions. You might have plans in place for your next step in missions. But what you might lack is developed opportunities for service—not singing in a nursing home at Christmastime but ongoing ministries that spring out of students' passions.

If you're a solo youth worker scrambling each week to put together a Bible study, see kids after school, run social events, and keep youth awake in Sunday school—not to mention planning that next mission project—you probably hate the thought of adding another task that occurs on a regular basis. But as you find ministries that grow naturally out of your setting, your adult volunteers, and your students' enthusiasm, you might find that moving students into service is one of the most effective, efficient places you can focus your efforts to grow your youth.

While you might be a dreamer with scores of ideas of how to plug your students in, your first job is to ask them what they want to do. Service opportunities that work long-term—without high maintenance, that is—are the ones that grow out of the gifts and interests of the real-live youth and adults in your church. If you have more than one student in your youth group, then over time you'll likely want to start multiple, varied ministries.

Before you feel overwhelmed, check these tips for any ministry you and your youth want to form:

✛ MAKE SERVICE MORE THAN A ONE-SHOT PROJECT. It's not that you can't do good in one-shot service projects. It's that your goal is to develop a core of kids committed to owning a ministry as their own. So aim to develop ministries that happen at least weekly. Why? If service isn't a regular component of a youth ministry program, youth won't make it a regular part of their lives. If it's a frill to you, it's a frill to them. But service is an essential part of their Christian lives. Weekly involvement increases a ministry's visibility and gets it on the family calendar along with lessons, clubs, and sports.

✛ FOCUS ON YOUR STUDENTS' SPIRITUAL DEVELOPMENT. Your youth are capable of doing great good in the lives of other people, but they still need coaching in their own faith. The spiritual growth of your youth and those they minister to is more important than flawless execution of a task.

✛ SHARE THE LOAD. No one person can organize multiple ministries. The only way ongoing ministries work is by finding other adult leaders who not only have a vision for what youth can accomplish but who also can excite others about the possibilities and open doors for them to serve. Forming a team of leaders for a ministry makes the workload lighter and rewards adults with fun and fellowship. One caution: Don't rely on students as the main leaders for a project. They're apprentices, not seasoned tradesmen. They need direction, supervision, and encouragement from adults who know where they are leading.

✛ START SMALL AND SIMPLE. An ongoing ministry enthusiastically done with a few youth cultivates a ministry mind-set in your youths more than a large, one-shot project with no follow-up. The programs you start can cost nothing—placing youth as helpers in children's Sunday school classes, for example, is free. And everyone has a Sunday school. While ministry tools like scripts and music cost cash, in the long haul involving youth in ministry is cheap compared to trying to captivate their hearts through entertainment.

Prep Session 4 (page 168) will focus on ways your students want to serve. For now, ponder some of your own ideas.

What ongoing opportunities for service do my students already have—opportunities that occur at least weekly?

_____

_____

What new offerings might they dive into?

_____

_____

_____

PUTTING IT ALL TOGETHER

You've got a trip to take. So focus on that for now. But you can also be mulling over now what you'll do later. And before you forget what you're thinking right now, answer this one question:

Of the four keys for keeping alive the experiences that take place on a trip—ongoing community, feeding, mission projects, and service—where do we want to start?

_____

_____

_____

Name another adult who can think about these things while your mind is consumed with the trip. Who can help begin to address all four of these needs?

_____

_____

_____

_____

CH.7

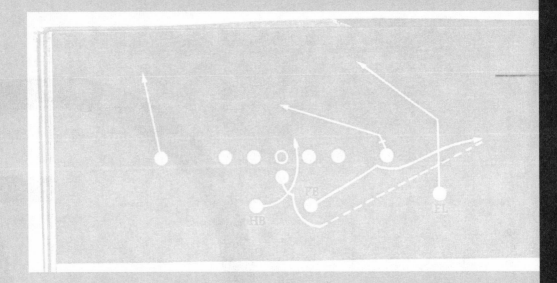

MAKE
YOUR PLAN

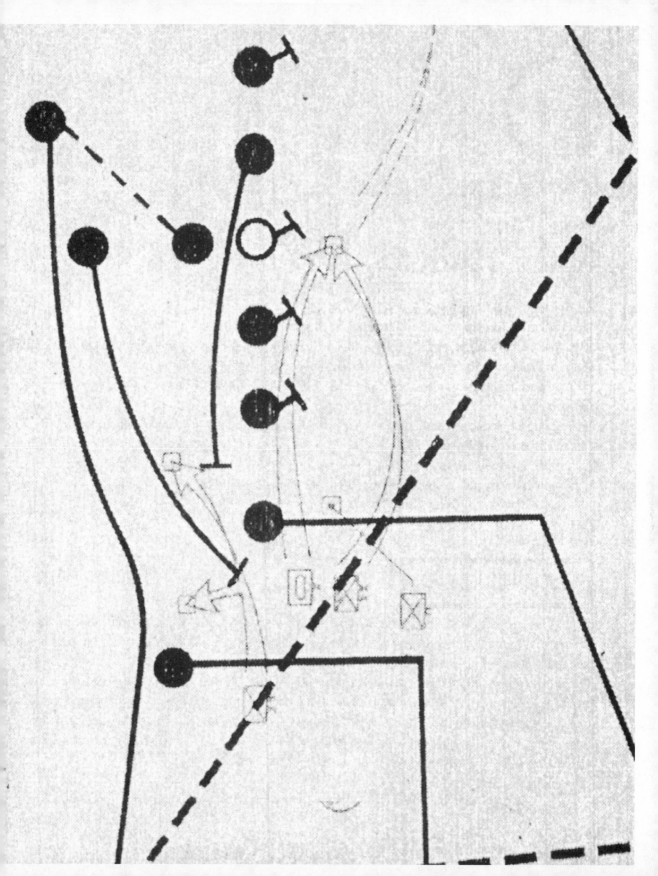

CH. 7

MAKE YOUR PLAN

PREP SESSION ①

If short-term missions were Star Trek, you could toss your students in the holodeck—a computer-driven 3D simulator big enough to create any virtual world you want—and have a perfectly accurate model of your project site. You could scan the environment. You could take a look at the inhabitants. You would explore their customs. You could practice all the skills you'll need for the trip. And when the time came to beam down to the surface, your students would be totally ready for a real visit.

Lacking a holodeck, your students can't know everything about the place you're headed until they actually spend time there. They could spend a lifetime acquiring ministry skills fit for a specific culture, but they don't have to go clueless. While nothing will replace the experience of getting to a mission site and living it in their own skin, the first thing your youth need from you to get ready to go is a picture of where they're headed.

SESSION OBJECTIVES

For groups in which participants don't know each other well, you'll want time in this first team get-together to meet and greet and start the process of bonding as a group. But your big goal is to paint a picture of where you're going.

Here's where you take everything you learned back in Chapter 2 and share what you know, expanding on what you've already boiled down for a brochure or presented in an informational meeting. Your participants already have a fuzzy idea of what they'll be doing; now it's time to provide details. You want to rally your group around an incredible adventure. You need to lay down expectations. You need to give your youth an overview of the trip. In this session they will:

 Participate in an activity that gets them thinking about where they're going.

✚ Talk about the details of the trip and their own expectations.

✚ Find out how Jesus is our matchless example in doing ministry.

✚ Pray about the work they'll be doing.

It all adds up to making a plan.

GET IT GOING

It's your choice: The activities in Prep Sessions 2, 3, and 4 can be thoughtful yet active—or they can tend toward the physically challenging. You may want to start stretching your group right away by practicing for your trip at a site close to home, doing here and now what you'll be doing there later. But your aim in this session to open eyes and ignite excitement for your project. Try one or more of these ideas to get your session started:

✚ **NEIGHBORHOOD PREVIEWS.** Your site might be close enough that you can actually visit. Or maybe you can find a similar site close to home. If you're going urban, you can serve at a soup kitchen, volunteer at a shelter, or take an eye-opening van tour of several organizations that minister to the needy of a city.

If you're headed for a rural setting, you could clean up the grounds of a country church. If you're going to a far-off cross-cultural site, look for a festival, fair, restaurant, or place of worship that gives your students a peek at their destination. Wherever you head out, chat beforehand about rude gawking, whispering, or laughing.

✚ **BRING DOWN THE WALLS.** If your students don't know each other well, start your session with an ice breaker to help a unacquainted group get to know each other. If you're looking for fun ways to get kids mixing fast, you'll find more than 200 ideas in *Crowd Breakers and Mixers for Youth Groups* (Youth Specialties, 1997).

✚ **UNIDENTIFIED FOOD-LIKE OBJECTS.** Missions often means new sights, sounds, and smells. Get a head start by serving everyone a plateful of unidentifiable foods—a small bite of each. Two rules are sufficient: Everybody tastes everything, and no one but you knows what the food is. Your choices can range from baby food to rattlesnake pâté to caviar, from unusual fruits to pig's ear (tastes like bacon with, well, an ear-like texture). Check ethnic or gourmet stores for the best selection. To heighten the adventure you can blindfold team members.

QUIZ TIME. Give your group a true/false or multiple choice trivia quiz about where you'll be going—and what you'll be doing and learning. If you haven't visited your site, doublecheck your facts with your hosts. Works on paper (you can score quizzes individually and give a prize) or on an overhead (gets good group laughs).

SURVIVOR STORIES. If you have students who have been on similar trips, pick a handful who grew a lot, and—here's the key—kept growing when they got home. Have them talk about why they went and what they got out of the trip. What was the best thing? The hardest? How did they feel when they first got there? What do they wish they had known ahead of time?

DINNER AND A MOVIE. Serve a snack—preferably one from your destination—accompanied by pictures or videos provided by your host group or drawn from previous trips you've done, even if those trips went to other sites. Highlight the unusual, but beware of making your presentation a thumped-up Mountain Dew commercial where everything looks cool and nothing looks hard. Beware also of nostalgia—sighing through the whole presentation in a way that means, "That was the best trip ever, and you guys won't ever be able to live up to that."

DO-IT-YOURSELF DIGGING. Distribute resources—Web pages, magazine articles, encyclopedias, a phone number of someone you've prearranged to be available for a call—among your group, and let students discover facts about their destination for themselves. Have students or group of students report back with three things they learned.

CROSS-CULTURAL OBSERVATION. Send participants out in teams of three or four students with an adult to a variety of fast food restaurants in various parts of a city—from the burbs to the core of downtown. Grill each group with questions when they get back: What kind of people did you see—race, age, sex, dress, economic bracket? How did people pay—with a buck and a half in change, a check, or a yuppie food stamp $20 bill? What were people in the restaurant talking about? How loud were they? Did they do anything you wouldn't do in public? How did people react when they saw you? Did you stick out in that environment—how do you know? Did you feel safe? Why or why not?

GUEST SPEAKER. Maybe your students won't believe you're a clued-in authority regarding your site. But you can always invite a credible speaker to tell you about where you're headed.

TALK IT THROUGH

Start this first processing session with an appropriate pep talk. Let your youth know that as you talk through some serious stuff in preparation for the trip, you need them to listen and participate. (Do you need them to speak up—or to shut up and listen when others speak?) And then paint the picture: Pull together the key points you pondered in Chapter 2 to tell your youth—

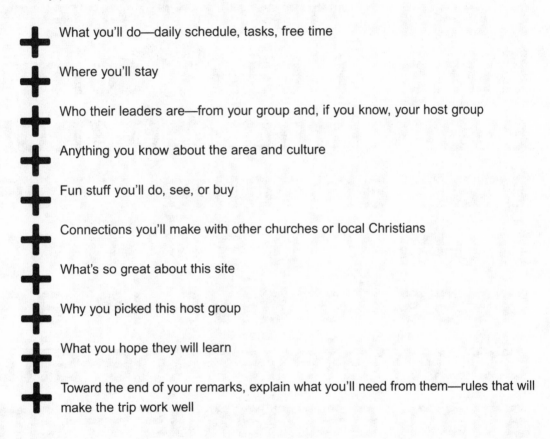

- What you'll do—daily schedule, tasks, free time

- Where you'll stay

- Who their leaders are—from your group and, if you know, your host group

- Anything you know about the area and culture

- Fun stuff you'll do, see, or buy

- Connections you'll make with other churches or local Christians

- What's so great about this site

- Why you picked this host group

- What you hope they will learn

- Toward the end of your remarks, explain what you'll need from them—rules that will make the trip work well

———— This project will be an adventure. I can't predict everything. I can't control everything. So more than anything I need from you a willingness to dive in and do whatever the situation demands—and do it with a great attitude. ————

That's an open-ended excuse to say at any moment of the trip, "I said this would be an adventure."

Take as much time as you can for an open-ended discussion of their thoughts about the trip:

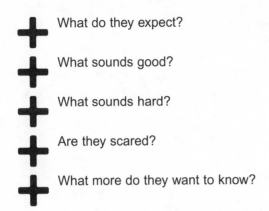

What do they expect?

What sounds good?

What sounds hard?

Are they scared?

What more do they want to know?

Promise your group that if they have any pressing questions you can't answer you'll find out for your next get-together. If your group is large, break into small groups, then gather back as a whole group to recap what was shared in the small groups.

GET IT FROM THE WORD

Whatever experiences your youth bring to your service project, you want them to beware of the attitude that they have the whole short-term missions experience figured out—that it's so easy and they're totally aware of what it's all about. We all come to a service project as learners.

After all—if you need ammunition to back up that bold statement—you're not the first people on the planet to do missions. People get doctorates in this stuff. Bible translators and many others dedicate their lives to getting to know small populations of people. Frontier missionaries go where the name of Jesus isn't known. Not too far back in church history, people sold themselves into slavery to take God's Good News to new lands. And about a hundred thousand other students will take part in short-term mission projects this year alone.

On top of those facts, we have an example of perfection we could spend our lives learning to imitate: Jesus is our matchless example of how to do a short-term project. He's the one we need to learn from.

What Jesus modeled for us was incarnational ministry. He didn't stay at home in heaven. He didn't merely mail a check to us poor needy earthlings. He came in person and ministered among us.

Again, the goal of these Bible studies isn't for you to talk at your students but to build teamwork and participation through group discussion.

Read John 1:1-14 and answer the following questions about Jesus and his mission. If you want you can pass out each question on a slip of paper to one or more youth—and have kids think about their questions—or find people with the same question and form a small discussion group.

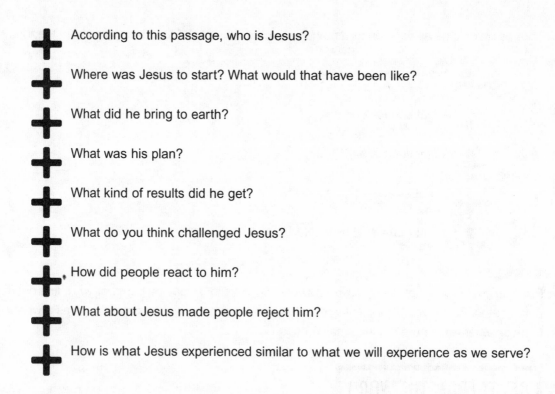

According to this passage, who is Jesus?

Where was Jesus to start? What would that have been like?

What did he bring to earth?

What was his plan?

What kind of results did he get?

What do you think challenged Jesus?

How did people react to him?

What about Jesus made people reject him?

How is what Jesus experienced similar to what we will experience as we serve?

Let your students talk, then round out their comments with any of these thoughts that remain:

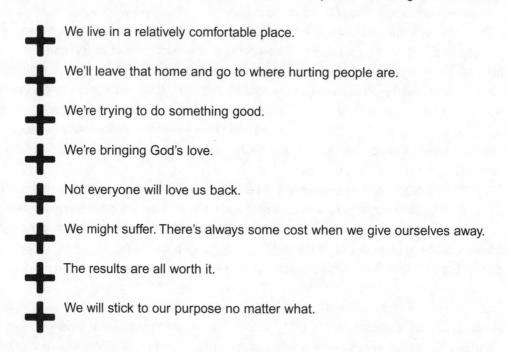

We live in a relatively comfortable place.

We'll leave that home and go to where hurting people are.

We're trying to do something good.

We're bringing God's love.

Not everyone will love us back.

We might suffer. There's always some cost when we give ourselves away.

The results are all worth it.

We will stick to our purpose no matter what.

All those facts mean that a mission project isn't an easy job. You can close your study time with a simple question for your group: Are you up to the task?

Some groups write a formal covenant for group members to sign—promising their total commitment to the goals of the team. If you choose to draft and sign that kind of agreement, think in terms of crucial elements of the trip—attitudes, fundraising, behavior, work ethic, commitment to pray, and so on.

PRAY IT UP

To end your session in prayer, break into small groups. One of the most meaningful ways to pray through these Scriptures is to say, "God, we are willing to go do the job you've called us to do. God, help us to do the job"—though students should be able to do so honestly. Set up a climate of transparency from the beginning. Alternatively, students can ask for God's help to be willing and for changed hearts.

You can read all of the passages and then pray or space the readings throughout a time of prayer.

When [Jesus] saw the crowds, he had compassion on them, because they were harassed and helpless, like sheep without a shepherd. Then he said to his disciples, "The harvest is plentiful but the workers are few. Ask the Lord of the harvest, therefore, to send out workers into his harvest field."

— Matthew 9:36-38

Go and make disciples of all nations, baptizing them in the name of the Father and of the Son and of the Holy Spirit, and teaching them to obey everything I have commanded you. And surely I am with you always, to the very end of the age.

—Matthew 28:19-20

But you are a chosen people, royal priests, a holy nation, a people for God's own possession. You were chosen to tell about the wonderful acts of God, who called you out of darkness into his wonderful light. At one time you were not a people, but now you are God's people. In the past you had never received mercy, but now you have received God's mercy.

—1 Peter 2:9-10 (NCV)

WRAP IT UP

Explain briefly what you'll be covering in the next three sessions—why you're going, how everyone can be servants, how to work as a team. Make any necessary announcements regarding forms, payments, et cetera.

TAKE IT HOME

If you choose, you can give your students an assignment to keep them thinking about how their attitudes will help or hinder the group during the trip. Some ideas:

PRAYER PARTNERS. Assign each person on your team another team member to pray for. Spend a couple minutes swapping prayer requests.

JOURNALING. Write a page on your deepest Christian experience—your biggest change. Or draw a picture. What happened? Why? Do a good job—take a half-hour or hour.

TRAINING LOG. Start a notebook describing "what I learned from this training session." Entries should be a paragraph long—what you learned, who you learned from, what you struggled with.

RESEARCH. Resources like libraries and the Internet will tell you about the people, politics, economy. Missionaries can tell you about the spiritual state of where you're going. Tell your youth to dig in. Make time in a subsequent meeting to share what they find.

CH.8

FIX YOUR

FIX YOUR FOCUS

PREP SESSION

You're driving in the inner city on a sunny summer afternoon. Side by side stand two decrepit houses. Shingles hang a-kilter, windows are broken, and graffiti decorates each house inside and out. At each house a team of 10 teenagers works to make the house fit for habitation. What's the difference between these two groups?

Members of Group A	Members of Group B
Tear siding off a former crack house	Tear siding off a former crack house
Roll up sleeves to facilitate tanning	Roll up sleeves to facilitate tanning
Toss a football during break	Toss a football during break
Pray before chowing down lunch	Don't pray before chowing down lunch

Saying grace before inhaling food doesn't say bunches about why students would spend a summer afternoon rehabbing an old house—and either of those groups could be from a church, Scouts, or a school. But let's assume that the grace-sayers are a church group. Is prayer before peanut-butter-and-jelly the only that thing makes their project Christian?

Way back in the early days of short-term student missions, few youth took part. Loads of adults thought students couldn't be yanked by their earlobes into any form of volunteer work. Now lots of churches participate. That's great! Besides that, volunteer service is often a graduation requirement in public schools. That's great too.

Many mission projects don't involve going door-to-door with the Good News about Jesus. The what of the trip often looks identical to the what of thousands of non-Christian groups. But there's a difference. When two groups are nose-to-nose, the distinction is what motivates a Christian group.

SESSION OBJECTIVES

By the time you're done with your first session, your students should know what they're going to do on their project. Now it's time to coach your students to think about why they're going. Your aim is to put Christ at the center of your trip—letting him direct, empower, correct, and applaud what you do. It means consciously aligning yourselves with God's goals.

You've heard how any mission project has three overarching goals—students' growth, others' good, and God's glory. At a minimum, you want your students to experience those things. But the take-home value of your project will be miles higher if they can name, understand, and even explain these colossal reasons for their trip.

You'll get at those goals as you focus on the spiritual side of your trip. Yes, everything about your trip is spiritual. Relating to God is like breathing. You do it all the time, but at crucial times you need to think about it. In your process of trip preparation, now is that time.

Your approach to this session depends both on the spiritual bent of your students and the demands of your project. You can:

✝ *Get quiet.* Go straight for a calm activity that gets at God's purposes for your trip.

✝ *Get active.* Practice for your trip and process the activity by talking about why you're doing your trip.

Either way, you will:

✝ *Do an activity* to focus on the reasons why you'll be taking this trip.

✝ *Talk honestly* with your group about their motivations for going.

✝ *Spot* scriptural evidence for working for our growth, others' good, and God's glory.

✝ *Pray* for God to pull us closer to him throughout the trip experience.

It all adds up to fixing your focus on Jesus.

GET IT GOING

Choose one or more of these activities to get your youth pondering God's purposes for the trip. You can also add in a worship time during which you focus on God's greatness and goodness. Any one of these activities can lead into a discussion and Bible study about why the group is headed off on the trip.

+ WHEN DID GOD FEEL CLOSEST? If you asked students to journal about their deepest Christian experience for Take It Home in the last lesson, give them an opportunity to tell what they wrote. Or take a few minutes to identify those experiences; then share them in small groups. Talk about this big question: Did any of those close-to-God moments happened in connection with serving?

+ WHY I WANT TO GO. Have each team member jot down his top five reasons for going on the trip. Encourage honesty—even if the reason a student wants to participate goes no deeper than getting a tan. You don't want faked spirituality, but you also don't want youth to fear expressing big godly reasons either. If you had your students fill out a trip application that detailed this, read highlights, keeping names private.

+ SPIRITUAL GOALS FOR THE TRIP. Have your youth list ways they want to grow while they're on the project. You could have them start by sending them off to be alone for 10 or 15 minutes to write three things they're happy with in their life with God and three things they're not happy with. (American evangelist Charles Finney called his variation of this exercise "plowing up the fallow ground." A fallow field is one lying unused. Before spiritual seeds can be planted in our lives, any hard, compacted dirt in our hearts needs to be broken up. We need to admit our need.) Then come back and generate a list as a group.

+ HEART'S HOME. Robert Munger's classic booklet *My Heart, Christ's Home* (InterVarsity Press, 1986) compares rooms in a house to parts of life we need to let Christ control. Get copies, read it beforehand with your team leaders, then make the book's lessons visual: Hold your meeting at someone's house. In each room put an adult or student leader prepared to lead a chat about what that "room of the heart" means. Break sstudents into small groups, rotating rooms every eight to 10 minutes.

✝ **PRAYER WALK.** Like a military reconnaissance mission, a prayer walk goes and scouts the terrain to see where God needs to act decisively. Take your group to your site if it's nearby or to a similar site in your area. Or you can set up a series of pictures around your meeting room as prayer stations. What needs—spiritual, physical, relational—do they see to pray about?

✝ **PRACTICE.** If you have a group with a strong hands-on orientation, your best starting point to discussing the goals of your trip could be to do close to home what you're going to do on your project.

If you're going to work with kids, schedule some time on Sundays or midweek to serve in your church's children's ministry.

If you'll be doing hand-on, practical tasks like rehabbing or painting, import someone who can teach your students the skills they'll need for the trip.

If you'll be sharing your faith verbally, students need to clear three hurdles. They need

✝ A living relationship with Christ

✝ Communication skills

✝ Practice

You can use your time today to plan an invite-your-friends social activity with outreach as its goal. Or you can use this session to practice skills you know they'll need for the trip. Here are simple ideas for building skills and experience:

✝ **TELL YOUR STORY, OPTION 1.** Use Acts 26 as a model for explaining your faith.

Acts 26:2-3—Paul introduces what he's going to say.
Acts 26:4-11—Paul describes his life before his conversion.
Acts 26:12-18—Paul tells about his conversion.
Acts 26:19-23—Paul explains the purpose of his mission.

Weave these points into one narrative—honest and free of Christianese—incorporating Scripture. Practice.

TELL YOUR STORY, OPTION 2. Write an explanation of your faith with these four points:

1. Describe a time in your life when God felt distant.
2. Describe what drew you to God and the commitment you've made to him.
3. Describe the difference God has made in your life, especially today.
4. Describe how you'd like to see God use you in the future.

Practice.

 EVANGELISM CURRICULUM. Use some or all of the sessions from *Live the Life Evangelism Training Kit* (Youth Specialties, 1998).

TALK IT THROUGH

You've probably heard the evangelistic question, "If you were to die tonight and had to explain to God why he should let you into heaven, what would you say?" You can ask your students a similarly blunt question about the trip: "If you were on our project site and someone walked up to you and wanted to know why you were here, what would you say?"

Take the next step with each of these activities by getting honest as a group about your reasons for going on the trip. The point? Get unity of purpose. As you head off on your trip, you need to know you're all kicking the ball toward the same goal line.

As a group, list on a board the reasons you're going on the trip. Keep it on why you're really going, not why you should say. A sort-of complete list might include fun, travel, adventure, see something different, hang out with friends, get away from home, grow in faith, learn servanthood better, get to know God, answer God's call, shop, get a tan.

Few reasons are outright wrong. Most reasons are fine in their place. Prioritize. Gently group these reasons into not-so-hot, hot, hotter, and hottest reasons for going. Get consensus. What's your number one goal as a group?

Whatever terminology you put on it, your growth, others' good, and God's glory are intertwined purposes at the top of the list for any mission trip. It's what you need for yourselves. It's what you need for the people you go to. It's how you get God at the center of your trip.

Transition into your Bible study by saying that putting God at the center of what we do isn't supposed to be hard. It's the right response to what God has done for us.

GET IT FROM THE WORD

Start by explaining in your own words how your deep desire—and the goal of those supporting your team—is that each member of your group grow closer to God through this experience. Then talk about your team's three big goals from Scripture:

GOAL 1: OUR MAXIMUM GROWTH

Give your group a look at what happens when we get close to God. Flip to 2 Corinthians 5:14-15 and have a youth read the passage:

> For Christ's love compels us, because we are convinced that one died for all, and therefore all died. And he died for all, that those who live should no longer live for themselves but for him who died for them and was raised again.

Ask team members what the passage has to do with your upcoming project and let them talk. Some points to draw out:

+ *We're taking this trip because Christ's love energizes us.* This passage applies to the whole of the Christian life, but the context around the verses shows how it really applies to a mission project. Verses 19-20 say, "God was reconciling the world to himself in Christ, not counting men's sins against them. And he has committed to us the message of reconciliation. We are therefore Christ's ambassadors." Paul is telling how God made us right with him, then made us his ambassadors—giving us the job of telling others about him.)

+ *We're taking this trip because we want to.* Christ's love motivates us from the inside out. We serve Christ because we want to, not because we have to. (Most translations read "the love of Christ compels us." That catches Paul's double meaning: We're moved both by Christ's love for us and our love for him.)

+ *Christ's death and resurrection had a clear purpose.* He died and rose so we would live for him. He loved us first. We serve out of gratitude for what he did.

So what else does our growth look like? What can we expect when we connect with Christ, putting him at the center of the trip? Look at any or all of these straightforward passages:

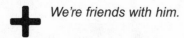 *We're friends with him.*

I tell you the truth, whoever hears my word and believes him who sent me has eternal life and will not be condemned; he has crossed over from death to life.

—John 5:24

 We depend on him.

I am the vine; you are the branches. If a man remains in me and I in him, he will bear much fruit; apart from me you can do nothing.

—John 15:5

 We obey him.

If you love me, you will obey what I command.

—John 14:15

 We say and show that he is great (we glorify *him*).

May the God who gives endurance and encouragement give you a spirit of unity among yourselves as you follow Christ Jesus, so that with one heart and mouth you may glorify the God and Father of our Lord Jesus Christ.

—Romans 15:5-6

 We seek his goals.

I hope in the Lord Jesus to send Timothy to you soon... I have no one else like him, who takes a genuine interest in your welfare. For everyone looks out for his own interests, not those of Jesus Christ.

—Philippians 2:19-21

We might not see those characteristics in our lives right now. But we want to see them develop on the project. We have another goal...

GOAL 2: OTHERS' MAXIMUM GOOD

The trip isn't just about us. What kind of good will God do through us? To find out, have a student read Luke 5:17-26.

> One day as he was teaching, Pharisees and teachers of the law, who had come from every village of Galilee and from Judea and Jerusalem, were sitting there. And the power of the Lord was present for him to heal the sick. Some men came carrying a paralytic on a mat and tried to take him into the house to lay him before Jesus. When they could not find a way to do this because of the crowd, they went up on the roof and lowered him on his mat through the tiles into the middle of the crowd, right in front of Jesus.
> When Jesus saw their faith, he said, "Friend, your sins are forgiven."
> The Pharisees and the teachers of the law began thinking to themselves, "Who is this fellow who speaks blasphemy? Who can forgive sins but God alone?"
> Jesus knew what they were thinking and asked, "Why are you thinking these things in your hearts? Which is easier: to say, 'Your sins are forgiven,' or to say, 'Get up and walk'? But that you may know that the Son of Man has authority on earth to forgive sins...." He said to the paralyzed man, "I tell you, get up, take your mat and go home." Immediately he stood up in front of them, took what he had been lying on and went home praising God. Everyone was amazed and gave praise to God. They were filled with awe and said, "We have seen remarkable things today."

Answer one question: When that group of men lowered their paralyzed friend through a roof to get him close to Jesus, what kind of good did they accomplish?

Three things happened. Jesus forgave the man's sins—spiritual good. Jesus healed his broken body—physical good. Jesus called him his friend—emotional good. When we imitate Christ's love for the world, they do good for others that brings people whole-life help. God is aiming for spiritual, physical, and emotional good for others.

GOAL 3: GOD'S MAXIMUM GLORY

The third purpose is the biggest of all. To get at that, share these two passages:

> ✛ See, darkness covers the earth and thick darkness is over the peoples, but the Lord rises upon you and his glory appears over you.
>
> — Isaiah 60:2

✝ For the earth will be filled with the knowledge of the glory of the Lord, as the waters cover the sea.

—Habakkuk 2:14

Then ask your youth two questions:

 How do you feel about being part of God's huge purpose of spreading his glory?

 How do you think that will happen—that people will see God in us?

Hmmm...those sound like hugely difficult questions, but they already know the answers. When people hear about God—either through our words or our actions—they realize his greatness. And when youth pursue the first two goals—their growth and others' good—the third takes care itself.

Have your students grabbed hold of the three goals of their trip? When they understand those facts, then they are on their way to catching a vision for the great stuff God is doing through your trip.

PRAY IT UP

Read out these references—having students look them up and read them for the group—or put them on slips of paper and have each student focus on praying one verse. Ask God to blow your mind with his love and pull you closer to him. Tell God, "This is what we want," or they can ask for God to work in their lives and to change them.

 EPHESIANS 1:17

I keep asking that the God of our Lord Jesus Christ, the glorious Father, may give you the Spirit of wisdom and revelation, so that you may know him better.

 1 JOHN 4:19

We love because he first loved us.

✝ ROMANS 8:38-39

For I am convinced that neither death nor life, neither angels nor demons, neither the present nor the future, nor any powers, neither height nor depth, nor anything else in all creation, will be able to separate us from the love of God that is in Christ Jesus our Lord.

✝ MATTHEW 22:37

Jesus replied: "Love the Lord your God with all your heart and with all your soul and with all your mind."

WRAP IT UP

Send your students off with any announcements about your trip.

TAKE IT HOME

✝ **PARENT CHAT.** Have students ask their parents what they expect from thetrip. What do they want their kids to learn? Even pagan parents have goals for their children.

✝ **FIVE MINUTES OF PRAYER.** Compile a list of four or five things team members can pray for each day or pick a theme for each week or design a calendar with one request a day.

✝ **PRAYER SUPPORTERS.** Line up people to pray for you, giving them specific items for prayer.

✝ **PRACTICE, OPTION 1.** Have each student practice telling a Christian friend who isn't on the team what it means to be a Christian. Ask the listener for feedback: Does what I say make sense?

✝ **PRACTICE, OPTION 2.** Encourage each student to start a conversation about a spiritual topic with a non-Christian friend.

CH. 9

GO
YOUR
SET

CH. 9

SET YOUR GOAL

PREP SESSION ③

Your youth surely need to know what they're doing on their mission trip. It helps most youth to grapple with why they're doing it. But if they aren't up to speed on how they're going to do it, you could be in for a miserable trip. You've already helped students glimpse the payoff they can expect from the trip—what their hard work will accomplish. But the quality of your trip—dancing through the highs and slogging through the lows—will be vastly improved if students ponder now the tough times that might be ahead of them on the way to their goal.

On a short-term mission project there's no way to predict what marvelous yet maddening opportunities might pop up—or what hardships might threaten to deep-six your group. The work might be tough. You might annoy each other. You might even suffer a small dose of humiliation as onlookers discover you're serving God. Only one quality will take your students through whatever they face and enable them to accomplish all they set out to do.

SESSION OBJECTIVES

If you had to pick just one word to describe the core of what you're doing on a short-term project, it wouldn't be travel. It wouldn't be vacation. It probably wouldn't even be build, dramatize, or evangelize. There's only one word that captures everything you're going to do: Service. Servanthood is the way Jesus worked in the world. Check out what he said:

"My food," said Jesus, "is to do the will of him who sent me and to finish his work."

—John 4:34

The Son of Man did not come to be served, but to serve, and to give his life as a ransom for many.

—Matthew 20:28

[Jesus,] being in very nature God, did not consider equality with God something to be grasped, but made himself nothing, taking the very nature of a servant.

—Philippians 2:6-7

If service sums up how Jesus operated, it also encapsulates how your team will accomplish its goals. While some adults would sooner teach beagles to leap over tall buildings than train youth to serve, don't underestimate the readiness of your teens to throw themselves totally and sacrificially into a cause. Servanthood is the key quality that will enable them to do whatever it takes to get the job done. It's how you'll do what you do.

During Prep Session 3 you will:

✝ Practice serving in a small but significant way.

✝ Talk through the good, bad, and downright ornery sides of serving.

✝ Be challenged by the example of Jesus as a servant.

✝ Pray for God to build servant hearts in your group.

It all adds up to knowing your goal of acting as servants.

GET IT GOING

Build time into this session to do a small but significant act of service together. You aren't looking to cause out-and-out pain but to stretch the students to try something they've never tried or that they've avoided. You might accomplish that by planning an unfamiliar activity. You might find that by choosing a challenging setting—setting up a shy, quiet team in a setting where they interact with people or assigning a team of grandstanders to a behind-the-scenes role. Or you might choose to bend gender roles—making the guys baby-sit and the girls drive the power tools or having the guys cook for your group while the girls clean up.

Servanthood responds to the real needs of real people. It doesn't have to involve launching into a new place. So you can make servanthood normal and everydayish by searching right around you for things your group can do. You won't find any shortage of nearby service projects. Check with your church, for starters, but don't neglect your city hall, schools, nursing homes, or other community programs and ministries.

Heads up: The most effective service you can do now is service you can keep doing when you arrive home after the trip. In this session you have a captive audience to pilot activities that can become ongoing service opportunities after the trip. Try these simple but effective ideas:

✚ **BUILD-YOUR-OWN.** Send your students in pairs or small groups in a dozen directions to let them invent their own service opportunities.

✚ **NURSERY TOY WASH.** How do you think all those germs get passed around? Think gumming babies and toddler spit. Scrub away with antibacterial hand or dish soap.

✚ **CHURCH PREP.** If you hold this session on Saturday, you can prep the building for Sunday morning services. You might include folding bulletins, washing windows, vacuuming, cleaning classrooms and meeting spaces, and setting up chairs. Pick a few tasks adult volunteers won't do. Make one option cleaning the bathrooms and watch what happens.

✚ **GROUNDSKEEPING.** Do the dirty yard work at church. Look around for manageable maintenance tasks to tackle.

✚ **BABY-SIT.** Send pairs or threesomes to help staff the nursery for the quarter before your trip. Get everyone at least two or three turns.

✚ **RAPID RESPONSE.** Let your pastor know your team will be ready to do whatever he needs done on a Sunday morning—on a moment's notice: ushering, set-up, clean-up, et cetera. Don't commit to what you can't or won't do.

✚ **SHUT-INS AND NURSING HOMES.** Develop relationships with people who need your friendship and practical help. Don't tease people by only showing up once in a while. Yeah, it's better than nothing, but you wouldn't want to be treated that way.

✚ **URBAN MINISTRY.** Get involved with ministries in your area that do everything from tutoring and childcare to cleaning, painting, and minor home maintenance.

✚ PRACTICE, PRACTICE, PRACTICE. Practice whatever you'll be doing on the trip.

If your group already serves frequently and happily around your church and hometown, here are a couple alternative options you can use to explore servanthood:

✚ FOOT WASHING. When Jesus wanted to act out servanthood, he knelt and washed feet. You know the scene:

So [Jesus] got up from the meal, took off his outer clothing, and wrapped a towel around his waist. After that, he poured water into a basin and began to wash his disciples' feet, drying them with the towel that was wrapped around him.

—John 13:4-5

Jesus did the job of the lowest servant of the household. He wiped grime from the feet of his dozen burly disciples. You can reenact Jesus' lowly act by taking turns washing each other's feet. A wash basin, some warm water, and a couple towels are all you need. Students may giggle, groan, or cry, but they almost always get the point.

✚ ROLE PLAYS. Think ahead to the trying situations you're most likely to encounter on your specific project. Write simple descriptions on slips of paper, draw them out of a hat, and have pairs of teammates role play the situation for the group. Do each role play twice. Have the student playing the team member react poorly the first time and in a more appropriate way the second time. Here are some typical scenes:

- ✚ A kid from the neighborhood clings to you.
- ✚ An old lady thanks you for what you're doing and says you're the kindest group of kids she's ever met.
- ✚ A homeless person sneers at your clean clothes.
- ✚ A stranger—a bizarre stranger—follows you around and won't stop talking to you.
- ✚ A child you're supervising disobeys and hits you.
- ✚ You're sick of working.
- ✚ A woman crumples up the tract you just gave her.
- ✚ A guy shouts you to the ground as you try to witness.
- ✚ You're trying to talk about Jesus with a group of people your age, but they ignore you.

Whatever the activity you choose, take time afterward to talk about what everyone has learned.

TALK IT THROUGH

If you've stretched your youth in any way, they're likely to have some ripe thoughts and feelings to share. Use these questions to talk specifically about your activity, either as a whole team or in small groups:

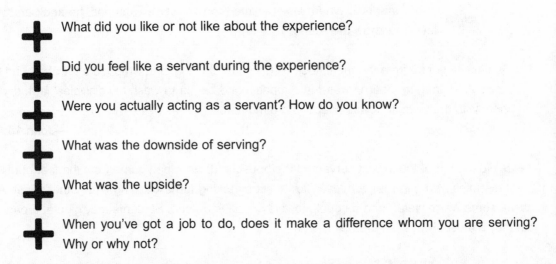

+ What did you like or not like about the experience?

+ Did you feel like a servant during the experience?

+ Were you actually acting as a servant? How do you know?

+ What was the downside of serving?

+ What was the upside?

+ When you've got a job to do, does it make a difference whom you are serving? Why or why not?

You've experienced a bit of servanthood—and talked about what it felt like. Now discuss what servanthood will mean for your trip. Start by asking whether the following people are servants and letting students explain their reasoning.

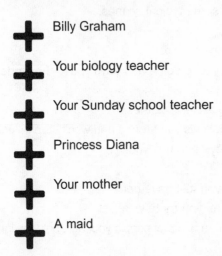

+ Billy Graham

+ Your biology teacher

+ Your Sunday school teacher

+ Princess Diana

+ Your mother

+ A maid

+ Mother Teresa

+ The president of the United States

+ Your youth pastor

+ A politician

Thinking about the answers, how would you define servanthood? What are you aiming for? Servanthood seems to require at least four elements:

+ **SERVANTHOOD IS ACTING FOR THE BENEFIT OF ANOTHER.** Think of the opposite of servanthood: selfishness.

+ **SERVANTHOOD COMES FROM THE INSIDE.** It isn't doing what looks good from the outside with a rotten attitude on the inside.

+ **SERVANTHOOD INVOLVES SACRIFICE.** Service can be riotous fun, but there's a price.

+ **SERVANTHOOD MEANS MOVING.** It usually means going somewhere—even if you only go to the kitchen sink. You get up. You wait on another person rather than having him wait on you.

The big news is that servanthood isn't our idea. It started with God. Jesus set the example himself.

GET IT FROM THE WORD

Introduce Philippians 2:5-8 by saying that servanthood isn't easy—not even for Jesus. This is one of the Bible's key passages about servanthood.

Have a student read the passage:

Your attitude should be the same as that of Christ Jesus: Who, being in very nature God, did not consider equality with God something to be grasped, but made himself nothing, taking the very nature of a servant, being made in human likeness. And being found in appearance as a man, he humbled himself and became obedient to death—even death on a cross!

Ask your team members to answer the following questions. Again, you can distribute these questions on slips of paper to individuals or to small groups.

+ What qualities did Jesus show in being a servant?

+ What limits does Jesus put on his service for us?

+ Why was Jesus able to do what he did?

+ Does Jesus sound like he was miserable? How do you know?

+ What happened as a result of Jesus' servanthood?

Here are some points to draw out:

+ Jesus had an absolute willingness to do whatever was needed. He saw humanity's ultimate need and came to meet it.

+ Jesus had an absolute willingness to go wherever. He left heaven to live on earth.

+ Jesus had an absolute willingness to follow the job to completion. He was utterly obedient to God. He made both small, daily sacrifices in ministry and the ultimate sacrifice on the Cross.

+ Jesus saw past what he would suffer to focus on what his sacrifice would accomplish. He had his eyes on the goal. Check out this cross-reference:

Let us fix our eyes on Jesus, the author and perfecter of our faith, who for the joy set before him endured the cross, scorning its shame, and sat down at the right hand of the throne of God.

—Hebrews 12:2

Servanthood doesn't always mean you're miserable. It isn't exactly the same as suffering. It's choosing to sacrifice for a higher good. It's searching for a different kind of fun.

One more topic to talk about: Make a list of the tasks your team is trying to accomplish—maybe in categories of Our Growth, Others' Good, and God's Glory. Then talk about what it will take to reach those goals. That's what servanthood will look like for your team. Some ideas:

+ SERVANTHOOD MEANS WORKING FROM THE HEART. God doesn't just want acts of service. He wants attitudes of servanthood. Review some of the good attitudes you've practiced during the prep sessions. Servanthood is where they all come together.

What are some attitudes you don't want to wallow in?

+ *Discontentment:* You'd rather be doing something else.
+ *Laziness:* You don't want to expend energy.
+ *Selfishness:* You want a payback for your service.
+ *Complaining:* You announce your suffering.
+ *Ignorance:* You don't know what to do and aren't willing to learn.

+ SERVANTHOOD MEANS WORKING HARD. Recap the expectations you have for work and ministry each day. Talk about how students can stay focused on the job. Discuss boundaries you'll set regarding work hours, getting to sleep at night, rest time, study time, play time, guy-girl pairing off, et cetera.

+ SERVANTHOOD MEANS ADJUSTING TO A HARD PLACE. Where you're going probably won't be just like home. You can expect differences in food, clothes, housing, hygiene, education, church, family structures, treatment of children, and life goals for starters.

+ SERVANTHOOD MEANS TAKING CARE OF YOURSELF. Jesus showed wise balance when serving others. During his day-to-day ministry he worked hard, yet pulled away from the crowds to rest and pray (Matthew 14:22-23). He rested so he was ready to serve again. A question to ask: *How is taking care of yourself different from spoiling yourself or indulging yourself?*

Wrap it up by noting that God doesn't expect us to accomplish any of these things alone. That's what we'll be talking about in the next session.

PRAY IT UP

To end your session in prayer, break into small groups. Tell God, "We want to serve with the same attitude Christ had when he served us," or to ask for his transformation. Your youth will remember the passages better if you space the readings throughout your time of prayer.

 ### MATTHEW 20:26-27

Whoever wants to become great among you must be your servant, and whoever wants to be first must be your slave.

 ### JOHN 12:25-26

The man who loves his life will lose it, while the man who hates his life in this world will keep it for eternal life. Whoever serves me must follow me; and where I am, my servant also will be. My Father will honor the one who serves me.

 ### MATTHEW 20:28

The Son of Man did not come to be served, but to serve, and to give his life as a ransom for many.

 ### 1 CORINTHIANS 13:1-3

If I speak in the tongues of men and of angels, but have not love, I am only a resounding gong or a clanging cymbal. If I have the gift of prophecy and can fathom all mysteries and all knowledge, and if I have a faith that can move mountains, but have not love, I am nothing. If I give all I possess to the poor and surrender my body to the flames, but have not love, I gain nothing.

 ### JOHN 13:4-5

So [Jesus] got up from the meal, took off his outer clothing, and wrapped a towel around his waist. After that, he poured water into a basin and began to wash his disciples' feet, drying them with the towel that was wrapped around him.

When you ask God to make you servants to each other and to all the people you work with, you can be sure he'll answer—in ways you can't even imagine.

WRAP IT UP

Any announcements?

TAKE IT HOME

Encourage your youth to practice being a servant at home this week. Try one of these ideas:

+ PICK-YOUR-OWN SERVICE PROJECT. Let each team member pick his or her own opportunity to serve at home, school, wherever.

+ PARENT SHOCKER. Do three things at home during the upcoming week to practice servanthood—above and beyond expected chores. Hmm...dishes, the lawn, baby-sitting, making a sibling's bed...

Before you send your students home, talk about this truth: It's often more fun to serve people you don't know than to serve your friends and family. Why?

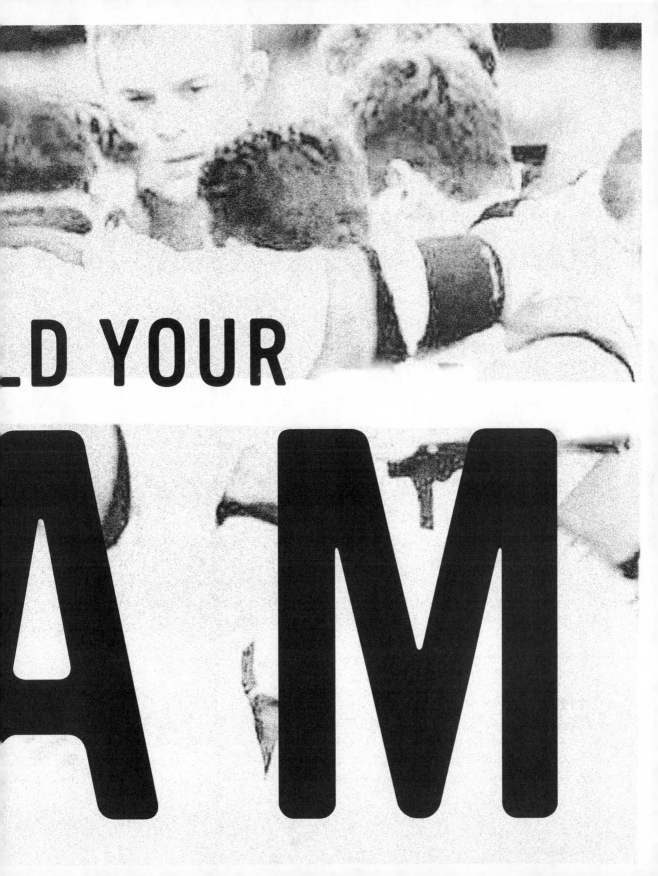

BUILD YOUR TEAM

PREP SESSION 4

The last day of your project has dawned, and you're packing up to head home. As you make the rounds talking to students, Marc, a sophomore, looks away when he sees you coming. You ask if something is wrong.

"It's bugging me that we have to go home," he says. "It isn't the same back there. This is the first time in my life where people have worked hard to get along. I don't have that at home. I've never felt that—even at church."

Missions takes us away from things and places we rely on for identity and security. Missions is often physically challenging. It's always relationally and spiritually challenging. A major part of what a student takes home from a mission trip is rooted in how he or she relates to the team. If she feels loved, she'll love the experience. If he feels left out of the group, he's at risk for being turned off to God and missions for good.

The community you create is multiedged. Community is the best thing about a trip, but it's the hardest thing to leave. Community is often what draws students to a team, but it will drive you apart when it's not working. It's a vital key to making the lessons of the trip real on the project, as well as taking them home. And if you aren't consciously, persistently working to build community—before, during, or after the trip— it will be tough to call your trip a success.

SESSION OBJECTIVES

By now your youth understand what you're going to do and why you're going to do it. They know how you're going to do it. Here's how you're going to do it, part deux. The message? You go as servants, but no one goes alone. This session helps you focus on building the teamwork now that you'll need later as you do your trip. In this meeting you will:

+ Participate in a teambuilding activity.

+ Discuss what went well during the activity—and what didn't.

+ Look at teamwork in the Bible.

+ Pray for God to pull participants together as a team.

The objectives all add up to building a team.

GET IT GOING

Don't be afraid to use your time-tested team-building activities that have worked wonders for you in the past; your plans don't need to be complicated. Here are some simple options to get your group thinking about teamwork.

If you've been going easy on your youth throughout your preparation, this session is a good spot to push harder. Provoking any issues of not getting along or working together now means you should have fewer issues to address on site. If you're looking for a tougher activity, check out the physically stretching yet easy-to-plan activities in the second half of the list.

+ **SILENT PBJS.** Use this simple activity for a meeting when you need to feed everyone anyway. The goal is for the team to work together and get a peanut butter and jelly sandwich. Spread out one or more blankets so that you have barely enough space for everyone to cram in and sit down. Two rules:

+ No one gets off the blanket.
+ No one talks.

Once everyone is seated and silent, give each person only one part of the lunch. One person gets bread, another person peanut butter, another person jelly, and so on. Don't forget plates, bag of chips, apples, cookies, drinks, ice, and cups. Hand over one knife for the entire group.

+ **TRUST WALK.** Divide people into groups of five or six. Blindfold everyone (except the Trust Walk leader) and direct students to line up and hold hands. The leader takes her group on a walk through the building and nearby community. Stay away from stairs, traffic, water, and cliffs.

HOME EC 101. Cook a meal together—something familiar but fairly involved, like pizzas with dough made from scratch. Everyone participates. Use dishes, cups, utensils, et cetera that have to be washed after the meal. Up the ante by adding appetizers and homemade cookies for dessert.

SCRIMMAGE. Pick any team sport or group activity.

GET CREATIVE. Plan and do a play for children or a skit or song about your trip for church.

PRACTICALITIES. Work together on anything that needs to be done for the summer—chores you'd get stuck doing if you didn't have help.

Here are alternative activities to gently but firmly push your group harder. Anything that's a bit longer or tougher than you'd like forces your group to work as a team. An activity that makes your group break a sweat also surfaces the ugliness now rather than on your trip. It exposes selfishness, anger, frustration, lack of determination—plus all the opposites of those qualities.

ROPES COURSE. Take your team on a ropes course—ideally, one with both low elements (for teamwork) and high elements (for challenge as well as practice cheering each other on). Ask if you can observe another group going through the ropes course before you sign on the dotted line. Watch for safety and skill at leading and processing the experience.

FLOAT. Canoe, row, or raft. Work hard and work together. Shoot for two to three hours canoeing, an hour or two rowing (or paddleboat racing), and a good chunk of a day rafting.

HIKE. Find a hiking trail that will give you a two- or three-hour challenge. Find an experienced hiker to lead.

BIKE. Most outings can turn into disasters, but group biking can be dangerous without practice. If this is your first group ride, rent quality bikes, stay off roads, and look for a paved or crushed limestone trail. Three to four hours should challenge everyone. Skid lids mandatory.

✚ **CAMP OUT.** One night is a romp. A couple nights gets to be work. Take two and work through some of these prep sessions. Play by the same rules—time for lights out, for example—that you'll have on the trip.

TALK IT THROUGH

There's a chance that your activity blew up. In fact, if people didn't get a little ornery you maybe didn't push hard enough. If people didn't get along, back up and role play how you can caringly handle each other's emotions—whatever you saw going on in the activity—anger, sadness, fear, frustration. Have one team member act out and another teammate or two respond in a way that will build your team rather than rip it apart. While you're at it, you can role play other emotions like homesickness and a bad attitude toward leaders. Your goal is to provide a vivid living picture of good ways to handle whatever the trip throws you.

After you've handled any explosions, move on to process your activity by talking through the points below. Unless your group is huge, do your discussion as a large group. Make a conscious effort, however, to draw out team members who tend to hang back and let others talk.

✚ What was your attitude toward our activity? (Did you feel enthusiastic, adventurous, negative, snotty, wary, scared, clueless, embarrassed, trapped?)

✚ By a show of hands, who was comfortable with the activity? How does being comfortable affect how much and how eagerly you participate? What would have happened if the group had participated in a different group activity—something that used other group members' strengths?

✚ How do you handle it when things go wrong or don't go your way?

✚ Who emerged as leaders? How? Would the leaders be different if we chose a different activity?

✚ What does it mean when someone is a team player? What does it look like when someone doesn't play for the team?

✚ How did we do making less-confident people feel part of the team? How can we do better?

What did you learn about yourself or someone else in the group?

Wrap up this part of your meeting by reminding your group that this whole mission experience is about attitudes. Colliding with new experiences challenges our thoughts and feelings. Bad responses can trash a good trip. Whatever we face, we face together.

GET IT FROM THE WORD

Especially if you've been doing lots of talking in the other sessions, make sure your students work as a team during this study. If your group is large, break into small groups. If your team is small, break into pairs or threesomes, assigning more than one Bible passage to a group if necessary.

Have groups work together to answer three questions:

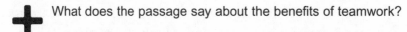 What does the passage say about the benefits of teamwork?

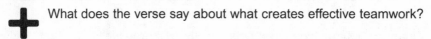 What does the verse say about what creates effective teamwork?

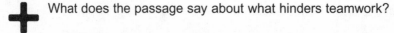 What does the passage say about what hinders teamwork?

Give adequate time for discussion, then have each group read the passage aloud and report to the whole team what its Bible passage says. Have your own thoughts ready so you can add points the students missed.

 1 CORINTHIANS 12:14-26

Now the body is not made up of one part but of many. If the foot should say, "Because I am not a hand, I do not belong to the body," it would not for that reason cease to be part of the body. And if the ear should say, "Because I am not an eye, I do not belong to the body," it would not for that reason cease to be part of the body. If the whole body were an eye, where would the sense of hearing be? If the whole body were an ear, where would the sense of smell be? But in fact God has arranged the parts in the body, every one of them, just as he wanted them to be. If they were all one part, where would the body be? As it is, there are many parts, but one body.

The eye cannot say to the hand, "I don't need you!" And the head cannot say to the feet,

"I don't need you!" On the contrary, those parts of the body that seem to be weaker are indispensable, and the parts that we think are less honorable we treat with special honor. And the parts that are unpresentable are treated with special modesty, while our presentable parts need no special treatment. But God has combined the members of the body and has given greater honor to the parts that lacked it, so that there should be no division in the body, but that its parts should have equal concern for each other. If one part suffers, every part suffers with it; if one part is honored, every part rejoices with it.

 ## MATTHEW 18:15-17

If your brother sins against you, go and show him his fault, just between the two of you. If he listens to you, you have won your brother over. But if he will not listen, take one or two others along, so that "every matter may be established by the testimony of two or three witnesses." If he refuses to listen to them, tell it to the church; and if he refuses to listen even to the church, treat him as you would a pagan or a tax collector.

 ## GALATIANS 5:22-23, 26

But the fruit of the Spirit is love, joy, peace, patience, kindness, goodness, faithfulness, gentleness and self-control. Against such things there is no law. Let us not become conceited, provoking and envying each other.

 ## JAMES 2:1-9

My brothers, as believers in our glorious Lord Jesus Christ, don't show favoritism. Suppose a man comes into your meeting wearing a gold ring and fine clothes, and a poor man in shabby clothes also comes in. If you show special attention to the man wearing fine clothes and say, "Here's a good seat for you," but say to the poor man, "You stand there" or "Sit on the floor by my feet," have you not discriminated among yourselves and become judges with evil thoughts?

Listen, my dear brothers: Has not God chosen those who are poor in the eyes of the world to be rich in faith and to inherit the kingdom he promised those who love him? But you have insulted the poor. Is it not the rich who are exploiting you? Are they not the ones who are dragging you into court? Are they not the ones who are slandering the noble name of him to whom you belong?

If you really keep the royal law found in Scripture, "Love your neighbor as yourself," you are doing right. But if you show favoritism, you sin and are convicted by the law as lawbreakers.

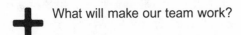 **PHILIPPIANS 2:1-4**

If you have any encouragement from being united with Christ, if any comfort from his love, if any fellowship with the Spirit, if any tenderness and compassion, then make my joy complete by being like-minded, having the same love, being one in spirit and purpose. Do nothing out of selfish ambition or vain conceit, but in humility consider others better than yourselves. Each of you should look not only to your own interests, but also to the interests of others.

Without unity, your team will pull in more directions than you have team members. Wrap up your study by asking your team for tight answers to these straightforward questions about functioning as a team:

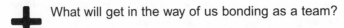 What will make our team work?

What will get in the way of us bonding as a team?

What would our project be like without a team—if we each went solo? What would we miss out on?

Close by thanking your group for the hard work they put into this session.

PRAY IT UP

For this meeting, stay in a large group for your prayer time. Tell God you want him to build a team that works together.

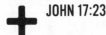 **JOHN 17:23**

May they be brought to complete unity to let the world know that you sent me and have loved them even as you have loved me.

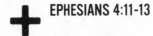 **EPHESIANS 4:11-13**

It was he who gave some to be apostles, some to be prophets, some to be evangelists, and some to be pastors and teachers, to prepare God's people for works of service, so that the body of Christ may be built up until we all reach unity in the faith and in the knowledge of the Son of God and become mature, attaining to the whole measure of the fullness of Christ.

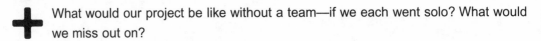

EPHESIANS 4:2-3

Be completely humble and gentle; be patient, bearing with one another in love. Make every effort to keep the unity of the Spirit through the bond of peace.

ROMANS 15:7

Accept one another, then, just as Christ accepted you, in order to bring praise to God.

COLOSSIANS 3:12-14

Therefore, as God's chosen people, holy and dearly loved, clothe yourselves with compassion, kindness, humility, gentleness and patience. Bear with each other and forgive whatever grievances you may have against one another. Forgive as the Lord forgave you. And over all these virtues put on love, which binds them all together in perfect unity.

WRAP IT UP

You're down to the wire. What do your students need to know or do? Doublecheck that everyone has a packing list—and understands what to bring and what to leave behind. Have your group repeat after you—at least twice—the time that you'll meet to leave.

TAKE IT HOME

YEARBOOK. If your students don't know each other well—big group, diverse backgrounds, drawn from different churches—compile a rough and ready yearbook. Include pictures and facts like name, address, phone number, interests.

PRAYER SWAP. Swap prayer requests for the frantic time before you go.

GUTSY CALLS. Assign students a partner to phone during the week for a check-in and encouragement.

SEND OFF. As you wrap up your training, you may want to plan a commissioning service, either as a team or as part of your main church service. Make it a simple send-off time—prayer, worship, and a short but rousing bit of encouragement from a pastor, elder, leader, or parent. Give yourself a break!

CH.11

THROW A

PA

THROW A PARTY

FOLLOW-UP SESSION ❶

You want your trip to stick. You want to see everything your youth learned during your project to last. You want their commitment to God and to each other to continue.

Guess what? The follow-up needed from you to help those excellent benefits happen starts as soon as your youth begin thinking about going home.

A few youth begin to mull their post-trip lives even before you've logged a single mile toward your destination. Months before the project starts they're already wondering what their next step is—and they might be asking if you have a plan.

Most youth wait until the tail end of your project to start thinking about home. And by the time you slam the door of your van or board a plane to head home you can count on all but the most in-the-moment youth to be wondering where life goes from here.

What's up?

PLANNING FOR THE END OF YOUR TRIP

You might plan to finish your trip with a big unwind—hitting a water park, theme park, or other attraction near your site or on the way home. But as you bring your trip to a close, you want to unroll three crucial pieces of your project strategy. You need time to sum up (that can happen on the last night), to wrap up (that happens best on the way home), and to regroup (that's the time you'll want together for two follow-up sessions once you get home).

SUM UP. Before you dive into cleaning up and whatever other activities you've planned to finish out your project, make time on your last evening to gather in a quiet place. Ask your youth and fellow leaders to answer this simple question: What was your most significant moment on the trip? It's an easy way to take stock of what everyone has gotten out of the trip.

Your aim isn't to make everyone sob, but you might want to bring a box of Kleenex just in case. Junior high boys might need some coaching not to laugh when high school girls wail.

Inconspicuously jot some notes. You'll want them later for your own memory, to prompt youth to share their trip once you're home, and to help your planning next year.

WRAP UP. Take time for a Do-It-Yourself Evaluation. Maybe you enjoy scribbling on the evaluations that camps and mission groups shove your way moments before the end of your trip, but most youth don't. You'll get more straight-up feedback if you simply ask youth and leaders what they did and didn't like about the trip.

Don't let the feedback go to waste, though. Whip out a notebook and jot some reminders you can share with your supporters back home and file for reference as you plan your next trip.

Some questions to prime the pump:

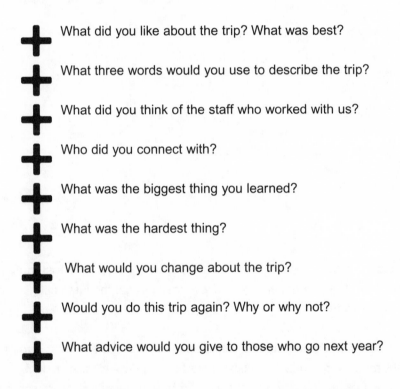

✝ What did you like about the trip? What was best?

✝ What three words would you use to describe the trip?

✝ What did you think of the staff who worked with us?

✝ Who did you connect with?

✝ What was the biggest thing you learned?

✝ What was the hardest thing?

✝ What would you change about the trip?

✝ Would you do this trip again? Why or why not?

✝ What advice would you give to those who go next year?

Summing up the trip and wrapping it up are two small follow-up needs. Here's a larger one: This chapter and the next provide you with plans for two sessions with your youth. The first focuses on regrouping and celebrating what you accomplished on your trip. The second asks your students to think hard about how they keep the cool stuff of your trip alive.

Plan your first meeting—your party and play time—within a week or two of returning home. Plan your second—the one to focus on making your trip stick—about a month or so after getting back.

SESSION OBJECTIVE

If you've been on a trip that takes a hunk of the summer—say, three weeks or more—you want to build at least a day or two of debriefing into your formal trip schedule. Go someplace where you can relax, play, and talk through the adjustment of going home.

Here's the plan for when you get home: Meet in a home or some other place that's comfortable and casual. Your goal for this meeting is to share God's joy in what you accomplished. Your job is to celebrate. It's one more shot for your team to solidify bonds before you scatter.

You probably don't need instructions on how to throw a party. But you can make this get-together more than an impromptu party. Don't unnecessarily pad your chat time or even your time in God's Word, because you want plenty of time for socializing. In this session you will:

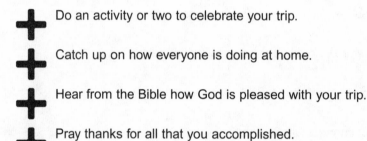

Do an activity or two to celebrate your trip.

Catch up on how everyone is doing at home.

Hear from the Bible how God is pleased with your trip.

Pray thanks for all that you accomplished.

GET IT GOING

If the youth in your group didn't have any social connections before the project, a post-trip party can get off to a slow, awkward start. Mix and match the following ideas to get the interactions going and give structure to the youth who want it.

PICTURE SWAP. Team members can spread out their pictures in various spots around a room. Other team members who want reprints can attach a sticky note to the print—with their name and how many copies they want. Each youth should put a cup next to their pictures so others can chip in a quarter or so for each reprint they want.

SCANNING PARTY. Alternatively you can have each team member who shot pictures bring a handful of their best pictures and have a photo scanning party. Burn a disc of photos for each youth and adult.

Bonus: If you've put together a PowerPoint presentation about your project, you can put that file on the disc as well as a self-executing Pack-n-Go presentation. Include the PowerPoint Viewer, which will run slide shows on computers that don't have the main software program. You can find the free viewer on the program disc or online at http://office.microsoft.com.

JUMBO THANK-YOU CARDS. Grab some light-weight poster board, markers, and other materials to make huge thank-you notes for your hosts, national Christians you met, for your church board, or whoever else deserves a warm thanks. Have team members deliver the cards by hand or pack and send in mailing tubes. While you're at it, make a thank-you card for each adult leader.

SKITS. Break into small groups and do impromptu skits reenacting your trip's funniest moment or other memories of the project.

PLAN TO SHARE. Don't make this party into a work session. But you can still start brainstorming ideas for how youth can tell other youth and the rest of your church about the experience. See **Take It Home** at the end of this chapter for ideas.

FIVE THINGS I WANT TO REMEMBER. Hand out nice stationery and pens and have each write A Letter to Myself about your project. Include ha-ha moments, significant lessons, relationships formed, and promises to themselves they don't want to forget. Have each youth address an envelope to himself. Put the notes in a safe place and mail them out in a couple months.

VIDEOTAPE COMMERCIALS. Roll a camera. Start recalling trip memories. Let the youth go weird. Ask them to tell their best moments and explain why others should go next time. You can also prompt them with the **Talk It Through** questions detailed on page 184. Play parts of the video when you share about your trip, and don't forget to pull it out to advertise your next project. The tape will be good for a groan when youth see how much they've grown.

AWARDS. A la sports team dinners, you can give an award to each member of your group—some serious, some goofy-yet-kind. You can present small trophies or medals or even items like personalized bracelets (available at stores like Things Remembered or online at www.thingsremembered.com).

MAKE A MEMENTO. Make signed T-shirts, buttons, potholders, a craft you might have done with little kids on the project—whatever will help your group remember the trip.

TALK IT THROUGH

The longer you've been gone, the more likely some on your team are experiencing a tough adjustment to being back home—a nonsupportive environment, a rough time at home, or just reentering normal life. Even returning from a short trip takes adjustment. Take time to check in with each student present, either in small groups or by wandering around as youth socialize. Some questions to ask:

✝ How is it going being home?

✝ What are you missing most about the trip?

✝ Who have you told about the project? What did you tell them? How did they react? Were they interested?

Again, write notes to yourself. Comments students make might seem obvious or incredibly impactful—but don't let them slip from memory.

GET IT FROM THE WORD

Grab this chance to stand up and talk straight at your youth—to congratulate them on finishing the trip and to thank them for what they've done.

Even the most mature Christian youth often wince when they try to imagine God is ever overjoyed with what they've accomplished. Take this opportunity to tell it to them straight. Jump into your talk by explaining that in the Bible passage you're about to read Paul has just told the people in Corinth how glad he is that they have enthusiastically given to early Christians suffering in Jerusalem. Then read 2 Corinthians 9:6-15...

Remember this: Whoever sows sparingly will also reap sparingly, and whoever sows generously will also reap generously. Each man should give what he has decided in his heart to give, not reluctantly or under compulsion, for God loves a cheerful giver. And God is able to make all grace abound to you, so that in all things at all times, having all that you need, you will abound in every good work. As it is written:

"He has scattered abroad his gifts to the poor;
his righteousness endures forever."
Now he who supplies seed to the sower and bread for food will also supply and increase your

store of seed and will enlarge the harvest of your righteousness. You will be made rich in every way so that you can be generous on every occasion, and through us your generosity will result in thanksgiving to God.

This service that you perform is not only supplying the needs of God's people but is also overflowing in many expressions of thanks to God. Because of the service by which you have proved yourselves, men will praise God for the obedience that accompanies your confession of the gospel of Christ, and for your generosity in sharing with them and with everyone else. And in their prayers for you their hearts will go out to you, because of the surpassing grace God has given you. Thanks be to God for his indescribable gift!

Tell your youth, "This passage is all about you." Talk through the points below—they don't need more than a phrase of explanation—and illustrate how you saw these truths come alive on the trip. What real-life examples can you offer from how you saw your youth and coleaders act?

+ **VERSE 6.** If we sow generously, we reap generously. When we give, we get back. What did God give to you as you gave of yourselves?

+ **VERSE 7.** God's goal is for us to give cheerfully. Giving isn't about being squeezed from the outside. When did you notice students giving gladly?

+ **VERSES 8-11.** God makes all grace abound. In other words, God gives everything you need to get the job done. How did you see that happen?

+ **VERSES 12-14.** People are thanking and praising God for your obedience. Who will benefit from what we've done?

+ **VERSE 15.** We are glad for what you did. Explain how the leaders feel about what the youth accomplished.

So what if you had a difficult trip? Admit that you had some rough spots. But for right now, focus on celebrating the good that happened.

PRAY IT UP

Just as it was your turn to talk, now it's your turn to pray for your youth. Give thanks for them—for the work accomplished, people met, lives changed, connections made to God and each other, and a safe return. Remind your youth that what they have done is a cause for celebration and giving thanks. Some great Bible passages you can pray for them:

 ### 2 CORINTHIANS 2:14 (NLT)

But thanks be to God...wherever we go he uses us to tell others about the Lord and to spread the Good News like a sweet perfume.

 ### PHILIPPIANS 1:3-5 (NCV)

I thank my God every time I remember you, always praying with joy for all of you. I thank God for the help you gave me while I preached the Good News—help you gave from the first day you believed until now.

 ### 1 THESSALONIANS 1:3 (NCV)

We continually recall before God our Father the things you have done because of your faith and the work you have done because of your love.

WRAP IT UP

You might have commissioned your youth before you left on your project. You can commission them again as they head back to their world. Make their send-off concrete by distributing candles to each participant. Light your own candle, then pass the flame to other adult leaders, who in turn pass the flame to the students. The symbolism of this candlelight commissioning is committing to be a light for God and to take the light of Christ into the world (Matthew 5:14, John 8:12).

Close your session by reminding students they did a load of cool things on their project—and that they can do the same things here and now. That's what your next and last session will be about.

TAKE IT HOME

Don't keep your summer to yourself. Get your youth front and center. Show off what they accomplished—their growth, others' good, and God's glory, of course.

GO MULTIMEDIA. Cut your youth loose to assemble a presentation that captures the guts of your trip. Weave in some text about what you accomplished.

HIJACK THE SUNDAY MORNING SERVICE. Split up the duties so no one person is overburdened in talking about your project. Five youth talking five minutes each, for example, fills up the time reserved for a sermon. Quiet youth can read Scripture, usher, and greet. Your whole group can share a worship song that was significant from the trip. Fill out special music by having trip participants doing their vocal or instrumental thing.

Have students write up what they want to say, then meet once or twice to screen and rehearse the talks. You and the youth will both be more comfortable if they aren't talking off the cuff.

HOLD A SPECIAL SERVICE. You won't have an automatic audience, but you'll get an interested audience. Provide food. After all, wherever two or three Christians are gathered together, a snack will be served.

TAKE IT TO YOUR YOUTH GROUP. Don't make youth who didn't go feel like spiritual morons. But make the most of your trip. Roll together the serious pieces you present for the adults with youth-friendly pieces. Both sides of the trip are crucial for your whole group to see.

SNACKS AND THE SENIOR PASTOR. If it would do your youth good to feel welcomed home by the church leadership, invite your head pastor to come for a special time of snacks to speak to and with the team. Even if he usually only shows up at a youth group function when it's time to fire or hire a youth director, it will do your team good to get the special attention.

CH.12

CAST THE VI

CAST THE VISION

FOLLOW-UP SESSION ❷

We aren't meant to go backward in life:

…to get teeth straightened—then watch them fuh-wang back.

…to get well—then get knocked over by a cold again.

…to lose weight—then balloon bigger than before.

…to grow up—then shrink back to fussing like a two-year-old.

…to get spiritually clean—then turn back into a mess.

The most scary, frustrating, out-of-control feeling in life is getting better in some way—then going back to the way things were.

As you continue to ease your youth back into everyday life, you want better for them than to slide backward.

SESSION OBJECTIVES

This session is all about where your group goes from here. You want to make it as easy as possible to get all of your team back together. If you take a summer trip, for example, it might be best to wait until early fall for this part of your follow-up. And waiting a bit isn't a bad thing. Meet too soon and you get irrational exuberance. Put your meeting off too long and you'll let the thrill of the trip die out.

This meeting is your opportunity to address some fundamental questions:

+ What are you going to do now?

+ What made the trip work?

+ How can we keep it going?

If you can figure out those answers, you can make the trip stick.

TALK IT THROUGH AND GET IT FROM THE WORD

Skip the opening activity to make time to talk. In this session you'll roll together your talk time and Bible study time. If your youth are reluctant—though they shouldn't be—tell them this is your payback for doing the trip. It's what you want most. As you ask the following questions, jot your students' responses on a whiteboard or flip chart.

+ How is it going being home?

+ What has changed? What hasn't—about you, how you act, bad or good stuff that you're into?

+ What made our project an awesome experience?

+ What did you have on our trip that made you spiritually strong?

+ What do you need to stay strong—to keep alive your sense of purpose and connectedness to God and the team?

Much of what you will hear should break into the four areas for further growth you read about in Chapter 6 (page 114). Point that out by labeling your list—showing which things fit in which area.

MORE COMMUNITY. Things we do to stick close to each other and to God, not just hanging out, but supporting each other's spiritual growth.

MORE FEEDING. Things we do to learn what God is doing in the world.

MORE MISSIONS. Things we do to tell people about Jesus through words and actions away from home, like trips your group wants to undertake in the future. (Yep—that's a narrow definition of missions, because missions also happens at home. But for this discussion, think of missions in terms of trips you can undertake in the future.)

MORE SERVICE. Things we can do to help people right here and right now.

Activities like shopping, sightseeing, tanning, and goofing around all fit under community, by the way. Getting away from home, going somewhere, and road tripping can fit under missions.

Of course God thinks you should have a good time when engaged in those areas. They're important to us, and they're important to him. Ask students if they can think of Bible passages that affirm us doing those activities. Discuss their suggestions. If necessary, you can read the following verses and ask them to match the text with the areas of community, feeding, missions, or service.

✚ Command them to do good, to be rich in good deeds, and to be generous and willing to share (1 Timothy 6:18—service).

✚ Let us consider how we may spur one another on toward love and good deeds. Let us not give up meeting together, as some are in the habit of doing, but let us encourage one another (Hebrews 10:24-25—community).

✚ But as for you, continue in what you have learned and have become convinced of, because you know those from whom you learned it, and how from infancy you have known the holy Scriptures, which are able to make you wise for salvation through faith in Christ Jesus. All Scripture is God-breathed and is useful for teaching, rebuking, correcting and training in righteousness, so that the man of God may be thoroughly equipped for every good work" (2 Timothy 3:14-17—feeding).

✚ Flee the evil desires of youth, and pursue righteousness, faith, love and peace, along with those who call on the Lord out of a pure heart (2 Timothy 2:22—community).

✝ Go and make disciples of all nations, baptizing them in the name of the Father and of the Son and of the Holy Spirit, and teaching them to obey everything I have commanded you (Matthew 28:19-20—missions).

✝ But you are a chosen people, a royal priesthood, a holy nation, a people belonging to God, that you may declare the praises of him who called you out of darkness into his wonderful light (1 Peter 2:9—missions).

✝ For we are God's workmanship, created in Christ Jesus to do good works, which God prepared in advance for us to do (Ephesians 2:10—service).

The conclusion? All of these things made your trip rock. And they're things God wants you to keep doing.

Be honest with your group. They can't go back right now, but if they're going to keep up how they grew together and the desire to do good in the world and spread the news about Jesus, then they can keep pursuing community, feeding, missions, and service here.

If you have options in place for continuing in the four key areas, remind them: "Community, feeding, missions, and service are how you keep your project experience going." Explain what the opportunities are, and encourage them to plug in. If you don't have opportunities ready—or if you want to expand what you offer—tell them you want to take time to brainstorm ideas to keep them growing.

MAKE A PLAN

If you're looking to develop new places for your youth to plug in, you could discuss options in each of these four areas with your whole group. Or you could ask students to break into groups to talk about the area that feels like it matters most to them.

COMMUNITY

One simple question should spark discussion: What can we do to build community—to make this a place where we keep growing together?

FEEDING

Start by giving a brief summary of the four areas youth can learn about and connect to real life:

✚ Global outreach—the frontlines of missions around the world.

✚ The persecuted church—Christians suffering for their faith.

✚ World hunger—including (but not limited to) the 30-Hour Famine.

✚ Evangelism training—find out how to verbally share one's faith.

MISSIONS

If you have students show up at a follow-up meeting, something went right with your project. You don't have to dive into planning your next trip for a while—you get at least a couple days off. So again, a few easy questions:

✚ Who thinks we should do another trip next year?

✚ Who wants to help pick and plan it?

✚ What could we do to help so our faithful leaders don't keel over from all the work?

SERVICE

If your project didn't take you far from home, then your options for ongoing service might be obvious; some of your youth might be able to return to your site to do the same activities. Or you might already have solid ideas for plugging your youth into weekly service tasks that grow out of their gifts and interests. If you want to run those ideas by your youth, you have a captive audience to hear your ideas.

If you're looking for ideas from the students, however, try one or more of these options:

BANG YOUR HEADS ABOUT YOUR PROJECT. What did you like? When did you feel like we were really doing something rabidly useful and significant for our growth, others good, and God's glory? What do we want to do more of?

FOUR QUESTIONS. These questions each address a different way a teen could latch on to a meaningful ministry. Have students pick the question that seems to fit them best, then brainstorm ideas. Work first as individuals, then spend time in small groups or with an adult leader for more brainstorming:

+ What have you seen others doing that you would like to join? You've seen ministries you think are cool and want to be a part.

+ What dreams do you have that you want to be involved with for God? You'd like to do it, but you're afraid someone will laugh.

+ What do you do best that you could use to help people get closer to God? Think music, sports, brains, ability to encourage, extrovert personality...

+ What need do you see right in your face that needs to be met? Think about home, school, work, friends.

NEWSPAPER SEARCH. Pass a stack of several newsletters from your church, school papers, community newspapers, your nearest big-city paper. Ask: What topic in these papers really riles you up? What do you care about? What could you do for your growth, others' good, God's glory?

FORCED CHOICE. You can gauge the interests of your group by asking these questions and motioning for youth to move to one side of your meeting room or the other for each question. Reminders:

+ Each answer is okay.

+ Don't go by what your friends do.

+ Just for this exercise, no one gets to be in the middle. Pick one side or the other.

Practice moving to one side of the room or the other with this choice: When you're babysitting would you rather change a poopy diaper or clean up barf?

Serious ones now. Take a headcount on each side and write down the result.

Do you prefer to—

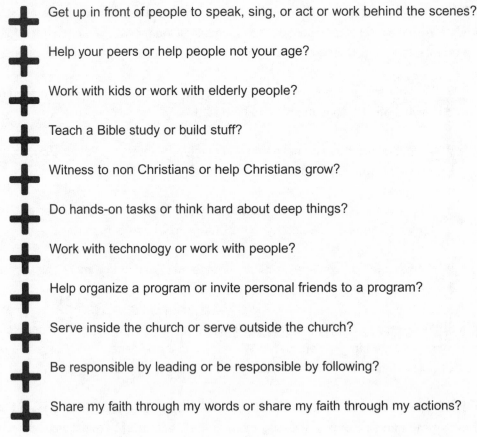

Get up in front of people to speak, sing, or act or work behind the scenes?

Help your peers or help people not your age?

Work with kids or work with elderly people?

Teach a Bible study or build stuff?

Witness to non Christians or help Christians grow?

Do hands-on tasks or think hard about deep things?

Work with technology or work with people?

Help organize a program or invite personal friends to a program?

Serve inside the church or serve outside the church?

Be responsible by leading or be responsible by following?

Share my faith through my words or share my faith through my actions?

Ask your students to think of three or four of those choices that generate strong feelings. (Jot key words on a whiteboard, if necessary.)

WHERE IS YOUR HEART? Ask these straightforward questions: If you could see God fix any problem in the world—besides getting some guy or girl to love you—what would it be? Another way to ask this: Where is your heart—do you want to see God working at school, at your job, in your family, at church, in some far-off place? And if that's where your heart is, how would you like to be involved? While answering that question won't yield any automatic answers, it will help you and your adult leaders point a youth to the right ministry.

PRAY IT UP

Give your youth a chance to say to God, "Yeah, that's what we want! We want to keep growing. We want to keep doing good. We want to keep glorifying God." You can use the verses from the Bible study, but here are a couple more:

ROMANS 12:1 (NCV)

So brothers and sisters, since God has shown us great mercy, I beg you to offer your lives as a living sacrifice to him. Your offering must be only for God and pleasing to him, which is the spiritual way for you to worship.

GALATIANS 6:10

Therefore, as we have opportunity, let us do good to all people, especially to those who belong to the family of believers.

HABAKKUK 2:14

For the earth will be filled with the knowledge of the glory of the Lord, as the waters cover the sea.

ACTS 1:8

But you will receive power when the Holy Spirit comes on you; and you will be my witnesses in Jerusalem, and in all Judea and Samaria, and to the ends of the earth.

TAKE IT HOME

As you wind down your trip meetings, explain to your youth how you will move ahead in these areas. Although you don't need to have concrete plans in place after this session, commit to them that you will follow through on helping them make the trip stick. Offer a timetable if you can.

And here are two books you can suggest—or give—to motivated youth:

CATCH THE WAVE by Kevin Johnson is a one-of-a-kind book on student missions and local ministry. It points youth toward getting involved in God's activities here, there, and everywhere—now and for their entire lives. Grab more info at www.thewave.org/catch.htm.

FIND YOUR FIT by Kevin Johnson and Jane A. G. Kise (Bethany House, 1999) is another unique book to help youth explore their giftedness—talents, spiritual gifts, personality, values, and passions—gifts that help them know how they can plug into God's work in the world.

Jr. and Sr. High students experience firsthand the impact they can have on the lives of those in need. It's a chance to meet hundreds of other teens from all over the country to work side by side to repair deteriorating homes, caulk windows, underpin trailer homes, repair leaky roofs and build hope in the hearts of those who are less fortunate. Through reaching out to others, Reach equips Christians with the skills and opportunities necessary to impact their world for Jesus Christ. It's not just about putting on a new coat of paint, replacing the leaky roof or hanging new drywall in a child's room. When it's all said and done, it's about our relationships with each other and with Christ. It's about Him.

REACH WORKCAMPS

2003   1.888.REACH.WC   WWW.REACHWC.ORG

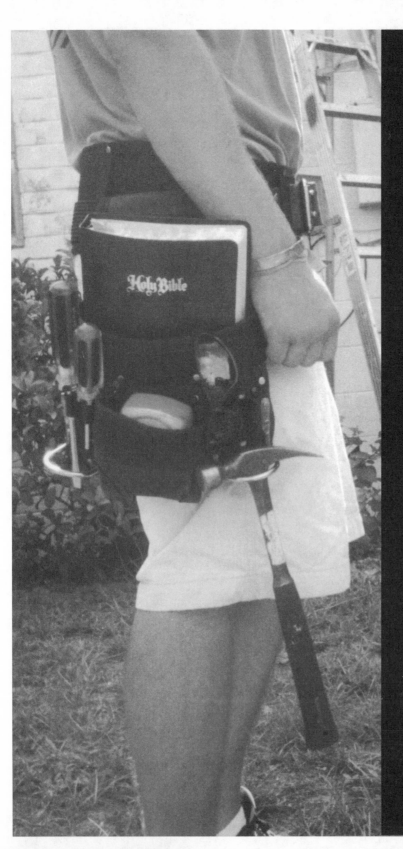

 CARE

 SHARE

 REPAIR

Ministries of Central Florida®

1.866.482.1041
www.impactflorida.org

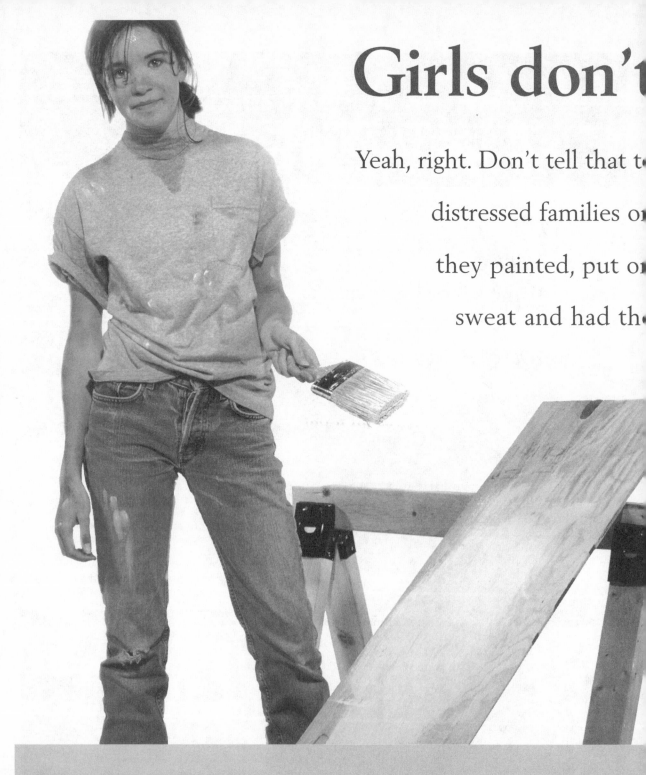

Girls don't

Yeah, right. Don't tell that t

distressed families o

they painted, put o

sweat and had th

A weeklong adventure. A lifelong

sweat, they perspire.

Caitlyn. She and her youth group spent a week serving

he Yankton Indian Reservation. In 95° temperatures,

ew roofs, installed weather-tight doors, worked up a

ime of their lives.

It was all a part of the Group Workcamps experience—

a fun, faith-building week of growth and adventure through Christian service. Join us at one of 72 camps nationwide for the #1 summer missions trip for church youth. Who knows, maybe the coolest part of this summer for your kids will be serving others.

At a Group Workcamp, your youth group can expect to:

- Grow leaps and bounds in their faith
- Feel great about making a meaningful impact on a family and community
- Serve others and build confidence and character
- Gain valuable skills through home repair projects
- Discover a genuine appreciation for what God has given them
- Have fun and meet new friends from around the country

W31-041

mpact.